The Small Garden in the City

On a flat blank wall at the end of a small courtyard in Chelsea the owner, Roy Alderson, has painted a brilliant trompe l'oeil, which gives the illusion of a fine flight of steps leading to a statue in a niche—but only the climbers and chairs are in three dimensions.

MADGE GARLAND

THE SMALL GARDEN
IN THE CITY

George Braziller, New York

Published in the United States in 1974 by George Braziller, Inc.
Copyright © 1973 by Madge Garland
Originally published in England by The Architectural Press.

Standard Book Number: 0-8076-0752-5
Library of Congress Catalog Number: 74-76646
Printed in the United States of America
First Printing

CONTENTS

The enclosed gardens of the Middle Ages resembled in miniature the fortified towns of that unsettled epoch. In this fifteenth century 'Paradise' garden, battlemented walls shelter small fruit trees and narrow beds in which bloom iris, lilies and columbines while Mary plays with her Child on a flower starred lawn.

INTRODUCTION

The subject of this book limits the garden to a small area enclosed within four walls; there can be no vistas, no elaborate planting schemes, all must be constricted in size and easy to maintain. It is infinitely easier to lay out a big than a small space, where every mistake looms large and every failed plant is at once visible. Special consideration must be given to the house and its immediate surroundings, of the design of the garden and the choice of plants but it is astonishing what variety can be achieved within a limited sphere.

The very word garden always has served to convey a number of widely dissimilar and varied images. To the Persians it was synonymous with paradise; to the French it conjured up a vegetable plot; to the Dutch symmetrical paths and regimented flowers; to the Scots an area high-walled against wind; to the Portuguese splendid steps and tiled seats; to the Moors

Gardens inevitably reflect the moral and social values of their time. The so-called 'romantic' gardens, inspired by the revolutionary teachings of Jean Jacques Rousseau, discarded the rules of symmetry and preached the virtue of all that was 'natural'. In practice a seemingly 'natural' effect could be achieved only by extreme cunning and kept in order by constant care. A successful example is this Penshurst garden created just before the war which has grown into a most delightful retreat.

an enclosed patio with water and green plants; to the Italians sombre evergreens and statuary; to the English smooth lawns and a blaze of flowers. How strange that the small atriums of ancient Rome, the vast formal designs of Le Nôtre, the curving landscapes of Capability Brown and the herbaceous borders of Gertrude Jekyll should all answer to the same name. But as Joseph Addison remarked there are as many kinds of gardening as poetry.

Not only does a garden describe many varied kinds of culti-vated enclosures but it also means something different to most people: to some it is an utilitarian annexe, to others an experience of pure pleasure. It was the conflict between these two atti-tudes that resulted in the following sad story of a town house

8

with a pretty and well-stocked garden of which the owners were justifiably proud. They were also possessed of an even greater treasure, a Chinese maid who was beyond praise. After a holiday absence they at once went into their cherished garden—it looked peculiar. Their Chinese maid had dug it all up and planted it with neat rows of cabbages—of a Chinese variety it is true, but cabbages. So much potentially fertile land gone to waste for a few useless roses, pansies and so forth, when it could produce much needed food, was inconceivable to the thrifty Oriental mind. Almost certainly if the Chinese inherit the earth the inhabitants would have enough to eat.

In contrast to the different descriptions and meanings given to the garden itself there has been a striking unanimity of opinion with regard to gardeners. Princes, poets and philosophers have all agreed that the gardener is a good man, and the Prince de Ligne went so far as to say that it seemed impossible that an evil-doer should engage in such a pastime. Certainly it is difficult to imagine gangsters patiently weeding a flower bed or vegetable plot.

It also seems universally acknowledged that gardeners are happy men, and most people would agree with John Evelyn that 'no man be very miserable that is master of a garden'. But note the word 'master'. All too many garden-owners are slaves, but of those who are successful it has long been customary to say they have 'green fingers'. Now a systematic examination of this phenomenon is being made and a new technique claims that plants have a nervous system, and that humans can communicate with them and assist their development by thought as well as by chemical means. A talk on this subject by Marcel Vogel of California on the English radio in December 1972 aroused much interest, particularly in connection with a community of some one hundred enthusiasts who have an experimental garden in the north of Scotland at Findhorn near Elgin. They maintain that they can communicate with the archetypal forces behind plants and with the fairies, gnomes and spirits, or 'devas', connected with each plant. It would seem we were back in the enchanted fairyland of Arthur Rackham if it were not that this theory has attracted several scientists, particularly some Russians, because they think that such experiments might lead to intercommunication with life on other planets.

Politics have played as much a part in the fashions of gardens as they have in other fields. The enclosed gardens of the Middle Ages broke out of their walls when the new ideas of the Renais-

Geometry has played an important rôle in gardening and for hundreds of years flowers and shrubs were subordinated to the demands of geometrical design. Such an architectural approach has much to recommend it in a town garden where nature has to contend with unnatural conditions. In the past many of the patterns had esoteric meanings and initiates could spell out 'love', 'duty' or 'charity' in the groups of pansies, daisies and pinks.

sance offered another approach to life. Political treaties resulted in trade agreements which brought in their wake new trees and shrubs. The great lawns, thought by many to be England's greatest contribution to the art of gardening, owe much to an Act of 1541 dealing with the game of bowls which encouraged the development of good turf. Credit must be given to the commerce of the East India Company for many of our roses, and to the international freedom of the first quarter of this century for permitting plant-hunters, such as Kingdon-Ward, to

10

explore the Himalayas and enrich our gardens with a myriad of magnificent plants, among them the rhododendrons which are so surprisingly resistant to town conditions.

The English have given multiple proof of their genius for gardening and perhaps it is not just chance that has given to their country an alternative name connected with a plant, for 'Albion' is said to have been derived from the white rose native to these shores, though another opinion links it with Dover's white cliffs. In no other country in the world has the modest cottage garden become an object of beauty still to be found in most English villages, nor can any other country show an equal number of small town gardens hidden behind dreary façades, unlike their surburban equivalents which flaunt their fancies for all to see. London, in particular, is a city full of surprises and it would seem that the present-day inhabitants carry out in their homes the Edwardian precept which insisted on the daily outer-wear of young ladies being dull and decorous but their underwear a froth of ribbon-threaded lace and muslin. All that can be seen is dull but all that is hidden is delightful.

It has often been pointed out in connection with fashion that during a firmly established civilisation the style does not alter. During the several centuries of well-organised government in Egypt and China, clothes and habitations remained much the same; the rectangular form of Queen Hatshepsut's garden, whose shape had been dictated centuries earlier by the irrigation canals, continued to be used as one dynasty succeeded another. In China a complex garden art, inspired as much by philosophical principles as aesthetic values, differed little during some twenty five centuries, and that authority on gardens, Edward Hyams, referrred with reason to Chinese gardening as 'massively stable'.

At other times, as in costume, certain elements recur in different contexts. Pliny's garden of the first century A.D. is strikingly like the French and Dutch gardens of the fifteenth and sixteenth centuries, and the classical tenets of Vitruvius found an immediate response among Renaissance theorists.

Fashions in gardens change more slowly than in architecture and far more slowly than in dress, but none the less reflect the moral tone and social aspirations of different epochs. The French garden with its elaborate *broderies* disappeared after the polemics of J. J. Rousseau spread the doctrine that only the wild is truly beautiful, and the savage gentle. What Ralph Dutton refers to as the 'ill-planned vulgarity of the Victorian garden' reflected the ostentation of a newly enriched middle-

A rectangular bedding plan was popular in the Middle Ages when it was usual to devote a separate bed to each flower or, more usually, herb. It is noticeable that the walls of this carefully cherished garden are bare; the town is a northern one which rules out the possibility of vines, and roses brought back by Crusaders were still great rarities, but where is the clematis so aptly called 'Virgin's Bower'?

class. The cubist designs of the twentieth century repeated out-of-doors the stark simplicity of contemporary interiors, both manifestations of that era's unsuccessful attempt to dispense with the inessential. Gardeners today pursue, usually with an equal lack of success, the ideal of a labour-free garden. There is hardly a weed so incapable of total eradication as the English love of the so-called 'typical' English garden described by Addison as 'a confusion of kitchen and parterre, orchard and flowers . . . mixt and interwoven with one another.' Nothing can be farther from this ideal than the possibilities of a town

12

In the Thirties undue severity of design began to be questioned and a house and garden of that period illustrates one way of achieving the best of both worlds. An orderly plan of paved area, path and neat beds is arranged near the house but the lawn leads away to a wooded copse. Optimistically a box maze is suggested on one side but was surely never executed.

The rectangular plan of this Brussels garden with its regimented tulips clearly states its date as the late Twenties when all frivolous fantasies were taboo and good sense equated good taste. There was also the shadow of a coming labour-shortage and the words 'labour-saving' considered as complimentary when applied to any decorative scheme.

garden in which design is paramount, trees often non-existent and flowers 'extras' often added annually at great expense by the local nursery-man. Only exceptionally strong-minded persons can successfully garden in a town and those who dream of a cottage garden have lost the battle before it begins.

In recent times the regulations regarding tree-planting, pruning and cutting-down, the use of front garden areas for parking, the often bitterly contested height of shared walls and dividing trellises are other problems which the town gardener must tackle before embarking on his own garden.

The haphazard arrangement of most of our streets bears witness to our excessive love of individuality rather than civic pride. The careful town-planning of Scandinavian countries with its emphasis on trees and the use of plain green lawns as contrast to bricks and mortar (or, more probably, concrete), plus the occasional happy addition of statuary or metal constructions, is sadly lacking in our cities.

The major eccentricities of our urban development have been held up to ridicule by Osbert Lancaster whose hilarious drawings are an apt satire on our fecklessness, but also offer serious food for thought. Yet there is much to be said for the diversity which characterises our streets. The modern fashion for gaily coloured front doors and of painting façades, once uniformly cream, each a different colour lends an interest wholly novel to once dull streets—which has been delightfully recorded in many water-colours by John Piper. Nevertheless it would be charitable to consider one's neighbours' front gardens and façades before planning one's own for much can be learnt from a study of the plants which thrive in the immediate vicinity—and errors noted can be avoided.

All specialists tell us that soils are predominantly either alkaline or acid and fall into four main types, sand, clay, chalk or humus and that it is essential to discover which the garden consists of before beginning to think of planting. There is however a fifth, the sour builders' rubble which constitutes the majority of town gardens. A comparatively simple test is to obtain a B.D.H. indicator which, plus distilled water, will give colour readings varying from pink for very acid, through green to blue for extreme alkalinity. But if an amateur is uncertain of his capacity to carry out this test a sure method is to send a sample of the soil for inspection to the Royal Horticultural Society (to which all good gardeners should belong), or to a competent garden firm for its opinion. Remember that

14

even a small garden may include different types of soil and thus offer diversity in planting.

A sandy soil contains large quantities of various materials of a quartz constituent and is usually deficient in plant foods. When given fertilisers it allows these to disperse rapidly to a lower level where the plant roots cannot reach and therefore the soil type requires constant top-dressing. A sandy soil also loses and gains heat rapidly, thus putting undue stress on the plants, so a certain amount of moisture-holding humus-forming material is required to provide a more equable temperature.

Clay consists mainly of hydrated silicates and other fine particles which tend to form solid masses which, though reasonably rich in plant food, are cold and sticky in winter and dry out quickly in summer. These defects can be mitigated by installing good drainage below the top-dressing with hydrated lime which must be dug in to at least two or three inches below the surface. Circumstances vary, but an average quantity of about three ounces to the square yard should have the beneficial activity necessary to break down any organic matter. Nevertheless constant hoeing is necessary if the ground is to be properly aerated, and it must be remembered that chemical soil conditioners have no food value and must be accompanied by fertilisers.

Chalky soils overlie limestone and are thin but excellent for all except such lime-hating plants as the *ericaceae* family.

A peaty, humus soil consists of decayed remains of former vegetation and can be very fertile if well cultivated but it is apt to get water-logged and become acid if not given sufficient lime. Of course manure and lime must never be given together and at least six weeks must be allowed to elapse between one and the other application.

Far too few people nowadays take the trouble of double-digging which any working gardener knows how, but is unwilling, to undertake, but this method of breaking up the second spit is one which will give real results for years to come. It is not usually necessary to lay a drain but sufficient to excavate trenches and fill these within two feet of the surface with clinkers and brick rubble, etc. A top-dressing of good soil is essential, and the excellent composts now available are well worth all they cost. Chemical fertilisers are also necessary and the town gardener must rely on lime, bone-meal, peat and other chemical products to keep the soil healthy and well-fed, but must beware of the rubbish sold as manure by itinerant carters which is composed of poor, pest-ridden lumps good only for propagating its own weeds.

The importance of forming a compost heap cannot be over-estimated. All vegetable kitchen refuse is useful as well as leaves (except those of the plane or sycamore) and grass cuttings are invaluable, both for the compost heap and as a summer mulch around roses. Remember that a compost heap must be in the shade, have adequate supplies of air and moisture and be aided in breaking down into manure by such additions as Adco. No trouble is too great to ensure that good soil is achieved before indulging in the expensive joys of plant-buying.

One factor which should be common to all gardens, large or small, rustic or urban, is the pleasure of scent. Many of the plants popular in this century have been bred for size and colour and have ignored the subject of scent. Perhaps our ol-factory senses have become dulled by the ceaseless onslaught of petrol fumes, but an effort should be made to include as many sweet-scented flowers as possible in a town garden to offset this threat. Mignonette is rarely grown nowadays, its modest habit and inconspicuous flowers ignored in borders bright with garish geraniums, dahlias and that garden menace, the all-seasons chrysanthemum. Tobacco plants with no scent should be rigidly excluded in favour of their perfumed relations and with a few exceptions, no rose however beautiful in shape and colour, should be without scent. Winter jasmine is a 'must' for every south and west wall. There are far too few hedges of the sweet-scented honeysuckle, such as those praised in London by Dr. John Hill as long ago as 1563, which was the favourite scent of Sir Francis Bacon, who wrote a percipient essay on the subject. He would have appreciated the delight of that pioneer of London gardens, John Claudius Loudon, who said that when the wind was in the west the scent of *Lonicera flexuosa* from his garden greeted him a quarter of a mile away as he came home to Bayswater, then a suburb, from London.

Two hundred years prior to Loudon's sensible and far-seeing plans for improving London's suburbia the author of the first English gardening calendar, John Evelyn, suggested that the city should be surrounded by square plots thirty or forty acres each, bordered with lime trees whose blossoms are so sweetly scented, and by fragrant shrubs. He lists sweetbriar, jessamine, syringa (philadelphus today), guelder roses, musk, lavender and above all rosemary to which he gives the credit of its perfume being wafted thirty leagues off the Spanish coast where it grows wild. *Mahonia Japonica* may have spiky leaves but its vanilla-sweet scent is a benediction on a winter's day when there is little else to give pleasure in a frost-bound garden. It should be planted near the door so that one can pass and enjoy it without getting wet feet. Recently, European musk mysteriously lost much of its scent but fortunately in the Thirties a species known as the Texada musk was discovered in the Gulf of Georgia which is heavily scented. Recently there has been a welcome revival in the popularity of scented flowers and the Chelsea Flower Show in 1972 was notable for several new species which were strongly fragrant, among them a fine hybrid tea-rose unromantically named Marjorie Anderson. The miniature lilac, *Syringa microphylla superba*, whose flowers are heavily perfumed has the welcome habit of blooming twice a year.

One first and last word of warning to all town gardeners, when a seedling or young plant dies, before blaming the plant, the nurseryman or your planting, take a good look for your neighbours' cats. They are the town gardener's worst enemies and where they live all plants are in danger, but there is no known prevention of or redress against them. The present generation would look with disfavour on the methods followed by our less squeamish ancestors who, according to a gardening manual of some seventy years ago, used wooden palings set with nails, and instruments of torture called Cat-teasers composed of tin plate with punched-out triangles so that the points made the surface impossible for pussies' feet.

Second only to cats is the nuisance of pigeons. Wicker bird-traps can no longer be procured from basket-makers and used with impunity in back gardens, and gardeners must continue to see their shrubs and garden furniture splashed and spoiled by the droppings of these messy birds. One day perhaps local governments will think it fit to clear our towns of these enemies of hygiene and health.

COURTYARDS

The remarkable transformation which has taken place during the post-war years in most town gardens would astonish the garden specialists of the early years of this century. As late as 1937 Miss Gertrude Jekyll noted that most London back rooms looked on to dingy yards and sooty walls, and thought that something ought to be done to ameliorate such a condition. During the Thirties there was a great fad for a country cottage and the small areas at the back of the town house were ignored. Gardens belonged to country rather than town life.

It was not so in the past. We know that in the twelfth century at the time of Thomas à Becket London houses had carefully tended gardens, though it is most likely these were devoted mainly to herbs not flowers. During the metropolitan expansion which took place in Queen Anne's reign the capital was beautified by a great number of gardens, terraces and squares. We read of vines, jessamine and other green climbers and shrubs growing successfully in the city near St. Paul's Churchyard, but conditions changed, the nineteenth-century urban development surrounded eighteenth-century London with a sprawl of built-up areas, hygiene was at a minimum and atmospheric pollution on the increase. As the twentieth century dawned the situation worsened and in 1909 the dense masses of smoke

The grotto garden at Gamberaia suggests an excellent plan for a heavily surrounded town garden, particularly one at basement level, concentrates its planting in large pots and gives interest to its walls by elaborate geometric patterns in stone and brick.

emitted from the chimneys of the buildings surrounding the Temple Gardens were a matter of public concern. It was considered that soot and dirt made town gardening impossible and one discouraged expert attempted to console a would-be town gardener by assuring him that at any rate turf grew well in a sooty atmosphere. Even the optimistic Miss Jekyll merely advised paving the few square yards of the back area and conservatively suggested vines, virginia creeper and a few ferns as the only plants likely to survive in an atmosphere poisoned by the fumes of thousands of grates burning sea-coal and, perfectionist that she was, considered it permissible to drop a few flowering plants bought from a coster's barrow in between the few hardy ferns. This is one subject on which the present era can be congratulated, for our cities are less dirt-laden since the smoke abatement campaign and the abolition of open grates which have made fogs a forgotten hazard. How surprised Miss Jekyll would be to see the hundreds of charming, if incorrectly termed, 'patios' which now are a feature of town

19

life and the innumerable beds of gay flowers which flourish in an atmosphere far purer than in the London she knew.

Miss Jekyll insisted that even the most modest scheme for the smallest yard should contain at least one distinctive ornament, a vase on a raised base, a stone *corbeille* of flowers, a fountain or a small basin, to form a focal point of interest. She would be delighted to know that her words have not fallen on stony ground but that thousands of small back and front areas have been beautified in much the same manner as she suggested, and that it is the exception rather than the rule to see an uncared-for town garden. Perhaps she might not have liked the forsythias which so generously spill their gold over London walls every spring, for she mentions only the *Forsythia Suspensa* in her *Gardener's Testament*, but surely she would have approved of the many magnolias whose fragile purity is one of the sights of many traffic-laden streets, as well as the hidden treasure of innumerable back gardens, and delighted in the camellias which bloom in profusion in many backyards, and in the wealth of clematis which covers once dingy walls.

Nevertheless, though conditions are so much better, if the area at the back of the house is tiny and receives little sunshine the transformation of backyard into courtyard has much to recommend it, particularly to those, too lazy or too frail, who do not wish to sacrifice to Runciana, the goddess of weeding. Any backyard lacking sufficient light for successful plant-growing should be considered a possible subject for this treatment which offers a positive improvement instead of the negative disappointment of a failed garden. But it is not enough to build a wall, pave the ground and add a couple of urns, ingenuity is required to give variety, and some unexpected and original detail must be added to give a spark of surprise. Above all there must be no hesitation, no half-way house, no looking back—or rather forward—to flower-filled borders next year. Nature must be subject to architectural tenets, and surface interest and sculptural detail must take precedence over plants, but once this plan is adopted and followed with firmness and discrimination, there is no reason why an unattractive back-yard should not become a delightful courtyard, for if there can be no botanical *bravura* there is much opportunity for originality in shape, detail and ornament.

The dichotomy between house and garden must always be the first problem to resolve. Attention must be paid to the spatial difference between the height of the walls and the width of the space and a careful plan devised which will give the

A nineteenth century garden somewhat similar to the Roman atrium seen in the previous page was recorded by Tissot when he painted his mistress in her St. John's Wood retreat. Here again the planting is confined to pots but instead of pebble and brick-work, the walls are ivy covered.

maximum effect both of variety and symmetry. Such preliminaries should be worked out with the help of an expert, for the amateur is usually ignorant of the manner in which harmonious proportions are achieved, though often painfully conscious of their deficiencies when it is too late to rectify the errors. Such a courtyard is more closely connected with architecture, of which permanence is a predominating quality, than with the changing, living organism of a flower garden.

A good prototype for such a conversion was the Roman atrium in which the proportions of the house and out-door area were closely correlated and the architectural style of the building was reflected in the pediment and classical columns which supported a loggia or decorated the walls. Most of these

21

carefully planned courtyards were devoid of plants: trees were not essential for shade as this was provided by the columned portico, and flowers were ignored. Spendthrift nature was not allowed to obtrude itself into these neat and tidy enclosures and Pope, when describing Timon's villa, remarked that there was no 'artful wildness to perplex the scene'. But, in another sense these Roman peristyles *were* artful for, small even by our modest standards—the garden of the Vettii in Pompeii was a mere fifty by twenty seven feet—they offer ingenious suggestions of how to convert a tiny urban area into a pleasant place of rest. Their lessons, together with all knowledge of the classical past, was lost in the Dark Ages and when courtyards reappeared after the fortified castle became an open villa, they were intended for the *manège* and exercise of the horses rather than the relaxation of the people.

Today this area, considerably reduced in size, is often no more than a parking lot for the owner's car, yet even this breathing space between the noise of the road and the calm of the house can have its utilitarian character softened and achieve a decorative appearance by careful attention to details. The ground surface should harmonise with the house façade and the steps, and a good stone urn filled with geraniums in summer and veronicas in winter will give an appearance of luxury to what is a plain necessity. An interesting surface is a great help in creating the impression that this often-vacant space is more than a mere utility, and such paving as the repeated half-circle carried out in square stone setts so often seen in France but less common in England, is only one of many variations which could be employed in this context.

The Dutch were among the first to develop the courtyard garden. Already in the sixteenth century land was scarce and valuable in the cities and even rich burghers could afford only a small open area at the back of their town houses. But with much ingenuity and care they made this into what Tom Coryate, a traveller of that time, called 'a delectable place of solace'. There were few flower beds, but if flowers were permitted they were planted in rows, one species to each bed, like soldiers on parade, each bed bordered by crisply cut box. The gardens were as neat and trim as a doll's with nothing fancy or romantic about them. A typical arrangement was of four paths crossing with a fountain in the centre, a cruciform pattern which dates back to the most distant antiquity when a square garden intersected by four rivers represented the garden of Paradise, a plan which continued to be followed in many small gardens for centuries. Today symbolism is as out of date as privacy yet it is fascinating to follow this first and simplest of garden plans (some say derived from the lines of the cosmic cross), from the second chapter of Genesis, through the Hindu vedas, the monastery gardens of Europe, the formal Dutch gardens to the backyards of modern industrial towns.

In seventeeth-century Dutch gardens the stonework and sculpture was carefully scaled down to the modest proportions of the yard, where its furnishings included balustrades, urns, statues and possibly an arbour with a table where meals could be taken. Moralists of the time disapproved of the in-coming fashion for flowers, which later developed into the fabulous craze for tulip bulbs, and many of these courtyards were planted only with an elder, a laburnum, or a couple of useful fruit trees trained against the walls.

Rubens's garden at Antwerp showed a development of this theme: it was composed of two adjoining courtyards, the first looking as if it had been imported from Italy so strongly was it influenced by Italian taste, with its chief ornament an important doorway through which could be seen a small garden with herbs arranged in symmetrical beds surrounded by a rustic fence. It was here that Rubens liked to walk in the cool of the evening with his much-loved second wife.

None of these Dutch gardens recall classical prototypes, they are an expression of a comfortable, middle-class way of life, not an extension of aristocratic dignity. The Dutch seventeenth-century burgher had no lordly forebears, no contemporary connoisseurs of noble birth to set a high standard of taste and luxury. In this matter, though resembling modern town gardens in size, they differ in spirit from the English garden which no matter how small, has behind it a long tradition of taste and elegance.

Nor had the Dutch gardens the same regard for privacy which until lately was an essential element in contemporary design. They were meant to be viewed from the canals which they bordered, therefore the hedges and walls were kept low, as Humphrey Repton noted when he visited Holland in 1764. He also remarked that the elaborately patterned beds, edged with dwarf box, were filled with coloured materials such as red brick dust, charcoal, yellow sand, green broken glass and various coloured ores, not plants. These beds were said to be the creation of the Elder Mollet, gardener to Henry IV who, finding the bare earth dull during the long winter months, invented this method of decoration. This fashion does not appeal to contemporary taste and is not likely to be emulated by even the most strict adherent to the notion of eliminating all plants from the garden.

Far earlier in date, though not known in Europe when Repton visited Holland, were the tiny gardens of Japan which also dispensed with flowers, but where privacy was greatly prized and the smallest yards surrounded by high walls. Some of these gardens are no more than three yards square, which makes a London backyard positively spacious, though we must remember that the inhabitants are considerably smaller than most Europeans. When an enterprising young firm of London dress-designers decided to sell to Japan they had to make their clothes in sizes 8 to 10, not 10 to 18 as in England. Most closely allied to these Japanese gardens in effect, but lacking their spiritual inspiration, were the geometric gardens of the sixteenth and seventeenth centuries composed of curiously shaped beds surrounded by clipped box whose designs were symbols of such abstract virtues as love, constancy and faith, somewhat similar to the elaborate embroideries then made by most women for household use.

No nation has carried the belief that art should subjugate nature to such an extreme as the Japanese, some of whose gardens totally ignore natural surroundings and dispense with all growing plants. Their famous Ryoan-ji garden at the temple in Kyoto has given its name to a special style which is carried out solely in curiously shaped stones and sand arranged according to the rules of certain mystical Zen Buddhist teachings. This Far Eastern forerunner of abstract art in the round dates back to the sixteenth century, nearly four hundred years before Western sculptors attempted to portray ideas, not human or animal forms, in stone.

The Japanese cultivated comparatively few flowers, it was the shape and design, the relation of each item to the whole, which formed the chief charm of their gardens rather than the trimmings of ephemeral blooms, and they admired their splendid paeonies and chrysanthemums singly rather than in grouped masses. They did, however, nearly always include a tree and cherished a cherry or a plum as much as for its blossom as its fruit. There was possibly also a tub filled with water for a few

An English example of an Oriental theme was successfully carried out by Anthony Denney at his Hammersmith house. Here an inscrutable ceramic lion presides over a miniature water garden crossed by a large pavement stone and a wealth of water-loving plants surround the small paved area sited directly beneath the back windows.

goldfish, and perhaps a miniature Bonsai—all useful ideas for a small, over-shaded backyard. Unfortunately the Japanese idiom was sometimes adopted in this country with more enthusiasm than discretion and metal storks, stone spirit-houses with upturned eaves and strange stones unrelated to their surroundings proliferated in many surburban gardens. Such East-West combinations often demonstrated the truth of William Robinson's sensible dictum that a garden should be constructed in accordance with the style of the house, yet some of these hybrids have been reasonably successful, and there is much to be learnt from the strict Japanese control over the diverse elements of their small gardens. There are many references to this new fashion in gardening in Edwardian books, such as the half-forgotten novels of Rhoda Broughton, when 'Japonaiseries' were the rage in aesthetic circles. The Japanese

The abstract garden was an inevitable outcome of the Cubist movement in the early years of this century but did not find its proper expression until the Vicomte de Noailles commissioned Guvrekian in the Twenties to make a plan for an uncompromising site at his villa on the Riviera (above right). Here the architect created a series of square boxes each filled with a separate species of flower, much like the mediaeval geometric garden, but suspended on a pointed cliff over the sea, not enclosed within comforting walls.

A later but far less successful abstract design was created by Raymond McGrath at Chertsey twenty years afterwards (below right). Here a paved area is broken up by a series of unfortunately shaped beds, circular, square and oblong, and a pool with a curved end, all enclosed in a white wall pierced by openings of different sizes. The bleakness of the whole conception is not sufficiently softened by planting and lacks the integrating force of an overall design.

style has continued to be popular in America where the influence of the Orient, particularly on the West Coast, is far stronger than in this island. It is a Japanese garden which has been chosen for the Unesco building in Paris.

The abstract gardens designed in the Twenties by devotees of Cubism are almost as much an expression of a mystique as the earlier Japanese examples and quite as rigid in their rules. One of the most successful was that of the Vicomte de Noailles in Paris, designed by Andre Véra, where different coloured gravels and stones alternate with beds edged with steel strips. Another, also belonging to the Vicomte de Noailles, is worth noting for the simplicity of its composition. The architect, Guvrekian, designed a pattern composed of identical diamond-shaped cement boxes, each filled with a different species of flower, which achieved an effect strikingly similar to abstract paintings of the time by Picasso, Braque, Juan Gris and Léger.

The high protective walls of the Middle Ages gave place to the open Renaissance gardens and many made extensive use of balustrading for marking their limits. This is a useful adjunct to the small town garden which is often seen, but the Italian fashion for trompe l'oeil is less often found in England, though the work of Roy Alderson (see frontispiece and p. 99) shows how successful this can be.

The device of separate geometric shapes was used again in the British Pavilion at the Paris exhibition of 1931, designed by Oliver Hill, which again solved the problem of creating an harmonious ensemble from a difficult site and its unrelated building.

In general, particularly for domestic use, such materials as cement and steel should be eschewed and the more tractable and familiar trio of stone, brick and wood relied on for ground coverage and enclosing walls. For the latter bricks are infinitely preferable to wood, they are more lasting, make a more attractive

27

background and give greater protection but, if they are relatively old, require the expensive attention of re-pointing which it is wise to undertake before beginning to lay the groundwork. Most urban gardens have their walls already *in situ* but if new ones are to built there is a wide variety of differently coloured bricks from which to choose. The changes in brick-fashions are almost as drastic as in dress: few people today would select the dirty yellow of the Science Museum in South Kensington so popular in the latter end of the nineteenth century or the hot red of Pont Street or Claridges, though Sir Basil Spence's choice for the fortifications he has built in Knightsbridge as homes for the Household Cavalry seem to presage a return of the latter unfortunate colour. Until recently the shade of dark grey known as 'London brick' was despised, but is now seen in many good-class modern buildings. Whatever colour is selected a fine quality hard brick is essential, cheap ones crumble and flake, and they must be laid in a well-mixed bed of sand and cement and have a top border of bricks placed cross-wise. Low walls, two or three courses high are best cemented, and terracotta walls should be painted with some cement paint to exclude damp.

Instead of a solid wall more and more contemporary gardens are surrounded by screens composed of bricks laid in such a manner that an openwork design is created. An alternative to the open brick construction is the new fad for pre-cast concrete sections in openwork patterns reminiscent of the Moorish lattice-work which is such a feature of Arab houses, and reached its apogee in the elaborately patterned wooden *moucharabias* of their balconies which shield their women from view but allow the fresh air to penetrate their apartments. These openwork walls can be effective if privacy is not essential, as it diminishingly is. The common way of life and the open-plan of American suburbia is becoming increasingly popular even in this conservative island, and the disadvantage of draughts is of no account if small plants are not part of the plan.

There are many methods of varying the overall design of the bricks. One of the most attractive is to sandwich horizontal fill-ins between every two lines of ordinary sized bricks. If space permits a serpentine wall can be thinner and use less bricks than a straight one: a curved form four and a half inches thick of average height will give as much resistance to pressure as a straight wall nine inches thick, but must have quasi-buttresses at intervals of ten to twelve feet. This shape offers interesting possibilities for the placing of statues or trees but is rarely practical in the predominantly rectangular design of city streets.

One of our earliest writers on gardens, Francis Bacon, maintained that the ideal shape of the garden should be square, and though many will agree with him, most town gardens are oblong. There are however several excellent methods of rectifying this defect. One of the most successful is to construct a balustrade, perhaps four or five feet high, according to the size of the area, across the width at a point which creates the required proportions. The concealed areas behind either side of the central opening of the balustrade can be used for a rubbish heap, manure or small frame, and no gardener needs to be told how precious and acceptable are such hidden corners. Bacon advised that a small garden should be encompassed on all four sides by arched hedges, for which charming conceit the evergreen *Japonica Aucuba* would be excellent. This device was often used in Holland and Belgium where the practice was to make every slender branch cross each other, then tie them closely together by pieces of osier so that there was no room for birds to nest. *Cotoneaster Simonsii* makes a splendid evergreen hedge decorative both when it flowers and when its red berries make a brilliant display. In Guernsey and the Azores hedges of hydrangeas are common, and there are few more beautiful sights than the miles and miles of blue hydrangeas, often over six feet high, which line the roads and divide the fields in S.Miguel, one of those islands in the Azores once thought, not without some reason, to be the legendary Atlantis. Although such flights of fantastic beauty are not possible in urban surroundings, if the rule of no plants is broken in the courtyard the hydrangea is one of the most reliable as well as the most decorative means of filling shady corners or lining dull walls. But water, and a lot of it, must be immediately and constantly available. Their name announces that they cannot abide dry conditions.

There are few sights more satisfying than a wall of greenery and though the sacred grove, which is its ancestor, has long ago been forgotten, the surburban hedge remains to remind us of something which has given pleasure to man for countless centuries. A courtyard devoid of plants can be rendered spectacular by a fine hedge, and a modern gardener could do worse than copy the great sixteenth-century gardener, John Evelyn, and settle for a hedge of clipped holly. For a higher wall hornbeam grows quickly and has the advantage of holding its gloriously coloured autumn leaves almost until the fresh

The familiar cruciform design is varied in this Moorish garden by a wide opening at the base of the steps leading to the conventional circular fountain placed at the intersection of the narrow paths—a plan as suitable to a Northern as a Mediterranean climate.

green of spring appears. The great *Cupressus Allumii* and or *Fraseri* will form a dense and evergreen screen, and though it is not often in town gardens that the legendary voice of the Lord talking in the trees can be heard, sometimes those whose backyards are too heavily shaded to permit flowers to bloom may find compensation in listening to a heavenly whisper overhead.

The cruciform plan of the early Paradise gardens with fairly wide stone paths, a small statue or bird-bath in the centre and the four corner beds filled with roses is hard to better. For winter decoration the beds could be edged with box, and spring heralded by groups of scillas and hyacinths, neither of which require annual replacement, planted around the rose bushes. If the principle of excluding flowers is strictly adhered to then the same plan of crossed paths could be carried out with the corners filled with evergreens. *Senecio Cornus alba sibirica* with its ruby-coloured stalks, *Viburnum Carlesii* or the golden holly would be a good choice. In some square gardens it is often advisable to vary the shape by placing a tree to shade a seat in one corner, with perhaps an elliptical bed of evergreen

A variety of paving and a difference of height give a sense of space and diversity to this small courtyard garden which dispenses with a lawn and depends on shrub planting and the fortunate possession of two large trees for its welcoming atmosphere.

shrubs on the other and to site the entrance on one side, not in the middle.

A courtyard requires the emphasis of one main feature, either a centre piece of a statue or well head, or a bench in the wall facing the house or perhaps a column in one corner. A sundial is decorative though all too often receives too little sun for it to be useful, but a bird bath brings perennial pleasure. A modern type of fountain in which a fine curtain of water flows steadily over a simple rim would give an ever-living shimmer of light on the dullest day. If the spatial measurements permit, a pair of urns on either side of the house door is

31

Water was and is one of the most magical adjuncts of any garden, far too often neglected in this rainy climate. In the Carl Milles garden at Tillhör a Jonah fountain, i.e. a whale spouting water, gives life and interest to a small pool. A similar example of contemporary sculpture is not without the possibility of most small town gardens and is one which would give a pleasure out of all proportion to its cost.

a practical method of introducing a few relatively trouble-free plants.

For the major consideration of ground surface the usual choice of York stone is both serviceable and pleasant if unbroken, but small uneven pieces are unsuited to an area which depends for its success on symmetry and the harmony of its component parts. Alternatives are brick or tiles which can be obtained in a wide selection of patterns and combinations. An attractive method is to use one of the many variants of brick

32

flooring, either laying the bricks in groups of two, three or four units placed in alternate horizontal and vertical positions, or to set them at right angles to create a herring-bone effect, or they can be laid in repetitive half-circles. The decorative terrace and marble inlaid floors, featured in so many Italian Renaissance paintings, are rarely practical in Northern countries but there is a great variety of stone available which, if not as picturesque as the exquisite floor in Perugino's *Miracle of St. Bernardin* with its white intersections containing grey squares enriched by lozenges of grey and black, can still be very attractive.

Dramatic effects can be obtained by laying dark and grey slabs alternating with black in diamond or lozenge shaped sections but plain dark and light squares are apt to look too much like a clinic. Another alternative is that of upended pebbles set into cement which, rather uncomfortable to walk on, can be decorative when used in a pattern. An unusually successful garden is that of an eighteenth-century house in Boston which has a court paved in carefully selected cobble-stones of a grey-blue and white.

Difference of level can add considerable interest to a small yard, even the unfavourable circumstances of being below ground level, in fact a basement, can be made an advantage if the difference is used to construct a series of shallow steps, not the breakneck type which usually leads from basement level to that of the actual yard. The whole aspect can be changed if the steps leading to the ground level are almost the whole width of the house, thus giving the effect of a stepped terrace as well as allowing a great deal more light and air into the lower-level room. The steps must be wide in relation to their height, each tread at least eleven or twelve inches wide and each gradient should have a riser of no more than six inches. Nothing is more mean-looking or accident provoking than a narrow step, and it is better to build three steps of four inches than two of six inches and make the horizontal lay as wide as possible.

The furniture for a courtyard garden must be in accordance with its architectural quality and should consist of stone table and benches, any objections to the discomfort of stone can be quickly disposed of today when foam-rubber cushions, damp-resistant and easily removable, are available.

In many of the early gardens, particularly in Holland, lead figures were popular ornaments not in the sober tones of the natural ore but painted in bright colours which must have had a somewhat garish appearance. Some coloured lead figures of the

Grandville's fantastic conception of the new music of sculpture in 1867 foresaw many of the abstract shapes which have had so great an influence on art, but so little on gardens, in the twentieth century.

eighteenth century are still to be seen in English gardens such as those at Tyningham near Haddington, but they reflect a vanished fashion.

Casts of classical statues in a mixture of stone and concrete, which is almost indistinguishable from the original stone, can be obtained now in a wide selection and are an obvious and possible, if conventional, choice. Here is a case where the old and the new could meet with mutual profit. Most contemporary sculpture looks best in an out-doors setting, most small outdoor areas require better furnishings than mere reproductions

An L-shaped area on two sides of a town flat has been converted by Kenneth Villiers into a garden which contains a large paved terrace and a small but deep swimming pool surrounded by terraced flower beds and shielded from the wind by a high wall and many trees.

of past fashions. Modern sculpture is of many kinds and some of the contemporary wooden or metal constructions, incorrectly described as art, could enliven what otherwise might be a dull backyard. Many amateurs who shy away from the more extreme variants would find sustained pleasure if they selected an example with care, and such an acquisition could be an original contribution to the environment, not merely a dull repetition of an already familiar object. These works are less difficult to find than is usually supposed, most art schools all over the country have a sculpture section from which the work of young enthusiasts can be bought for a relatively modest sum. Not every amateur patron can be sure of acquiring an early example of a future Henry Moore, but there is always the possibility

That twentieth-century garden status-symbol, the swimming pool, has been given total accep-
tance in David Hockney's brilliant picture of Nick Wilder in his pool at his Californian
house. The static beauty of the building, the aquamarine glitter of the water and the complete
assurance of the owner make an unforgettable picture of the Successful Sixties. 36

of discovering new talent and the fun of backing one's own fancy.

It is strange that the fashion for wooden statues has not been revived. These were a great feature of Tudor gardens and at Whitehall Elizabeth I had thirty-four carved wooden beasts seated on wooden pillars holding aloft weather vanes. Though today one cannot envisage quite such a consortium of creatures in one garden a single example would be delightful. Some people have been lucky enough to find figures from a fair merry-go-round, or a ship's figure-head and these are real treasures, but contemporary wooden statues are rarely seen. Yet one of Zadkin's most successful works was a statue made of oak which was the glory of a Sussex garden in the early Thirties.

It is also curious that the use of mineralogical or geological specimens is so rare among garden decorations. Large pieces of Derbyshire spar or strangely shaped stones would look dramatic. One nineteenth-century English gardener did suggest basalt from the Giant's Causeway as a garden ornament, but such items are rarely seen. More familiar are the giant clam shells brought by sailors from the Far East which are still to be seen in cottage front gardens and are now eagerly sought after by town dwellers. Another suggestion from the Orient was the broken porcelain once used as a surface ornament for pots and urns but now longer seen, and one has to go to the Temple of the Sunrise at Bangkok to realise the full horror of this happily extinct fashion.

THE OUTDOOR ROOM

The conception of the garden as an outdoor room, an extension of the house rather than a separate entity, has been extensively developed in Italy from Roman times to this day. An intimate connection between house and garden was part of the classical tradition and a garden-room was included in the residences of most well-to-do Roman citizens. The average house was built round an open square, or atrium, on to which the main rooms opened thus forming a continuation of the living space, and it was here that the family took their meals in fine weather. Like the Roman house it was practical and unromantic, its lines straight and the proportions of the columns supporting the roof of the loggia repeated those of the main building which conformed to the antique ideal of one tenth thickness to height. In the centre of the open space a fountain usually played, as much for use as for pleasure, stone seats were placed along the wall and a colonnade gave shelter from the sun. At Sallust's house at Pompeii the garden-room had the wall opposite the house painted with trees at whose base some low shrubs were planted. There was a fountain against a wall and at the end of

An idealised garden room was created in the first century AD in Livia's villa at Prima Porta near Rome. It shows a decorative balustrade with clumps of flowers in front and trees behind except for one framed by a central recess. The whole design appears to be raised from the ground by a double step.

In the auditorium of Mycene at Rome a painted arbour has a shallow fountain as its focal point framed by a stone balustrade pierced with decorative openings and birds perched in the branches of the trees behind.

the brief walk a vine-covered arbour and a table beneath with turf seats beside it.

An idealised version of a Roman garden can be seen in Livia's painted room at Prima Porta near Rome. This shows it surrounded by a low stone balustrade with four recesses in each of which is planted a different kind of tree, in front is a grass path, or *ambulatio*, its edges decorated with such small plants as violets, harts-tongue ferns, roses and iris, all shown blooming together, a fancy for all seasons, a painted Chelsea flower show in miniature. On either side of the small enclosure fountains play, and in the centre is a statue of a male reclining figure. This last may be beyond the scope or purse of the average town gardener but otherwise the plan would be easy to reconstruct with live plants replacing their painted predecessors.

Another painted Pompeiian garden shows a series of four arbours complete with birds, shrubs flanked with urns, and behind them ever-greens cut into curious shapes. Much attention was paid in Roman times to the history and method of cutting evergreens, or tree-barbering, which in due course led to the craze for topiary in succeeding centuries.

Topiary must be divided into two categories. Either it can be purely utilitarian and form walls around the garden or an arbour, or it can be merely ornamental. Yew, box, holly and cypress have been favourites for this form of garden ornamentation, and slow-growing but long-lasting yew can develop into almost impenetrable buttresses. One tree alone has been known to form an arbour fourteen feet square and eighteen feet high. One of the few happy results of the present-day labour shortage is that the hideous habit of barbering trees into grotesque shapes has been discontinued, though recently no less a garden expert than Miles Hadfield has attempted to recreate an interest in this most unnatural garden ornament. His record of its development is of more historical interest than for practical use in contemporary gardens. Still there are masochists in gardens as well as in other places, and many amateurs may be spurred on to destroy the leisure of their weekends by torturing plants into the curious forms similar to those created by professional gardeners in the past.

With the exception of topiary all was logical and rational in

A narrow town garden achieves the maximum seclusion with high creeper-clad walls. Steps at the far end and a fountain give year-round interest, colour is added in summer by a few bedding plants and permanent seating achieved by a group of decorative ironwork chairs and a table.

the Roman garden which was arranged for human comfort and convenience rather than a place in which to grow plants and flowers. When Horace suggested that a garden should be an inspiration and contribute to spiritual refreshment it was a new idea totally out of sympathy with contemporary thought.

It was not until the seventeenth century when that great traveller and gardener John Parkinson wrote a book called *The Earthly Paradise* that a plea was put forward that gardens should be for delight rather than for use, a concept which did not find its complete fulfilment until nearly two hundred years later when the romantic *jardin anglais* combined the picturesque with the poetical.

The Roman, and later the Italian, small garden-rooms relied on architectural harmony and careful detail for their effects, rather than flowers, but great importance was attached to the meanings of those few plants permitted within the precincts. Surely it is a great loss to-day that we are so little aware of the wealth of legend and association connected with plants. They no longer tell a story: the sober ivy does not instantly recall the orgies of licentious Dionysos; it is forgotten that the myrtle symbolises the combination of love with pleasure, and that the laurel, later a sign of the victor's prowesss, was brought as an emblem of peace by Livia's white fowl. The rose, sacred to Aphrodite, is still accepted as the messenger of true love, but to most people today plants recall horticultural or geographical information rather than colourful stories of mythical gods.

The tradition of the Roman outdoor room and the Roman love of gardens was carried by the legionaries across Europe and in towns built by the Roman conquerors in Britain most of the houses had their own gardens. In the Auvergne a Gallo-Roman bishop of the fourth century has left a delightful description of his house near Clermont, which he built at a time when barbarian tribes were begining to over-run the Roman provinces. Sidonious speaks with pride of his two dining rooms, one indoors with an open hearth for winter, and one half out of doors for summer, conveniently placed on the shady side of the house where there was a loggia and a colonnaire.

The medieval version of the garden-room was the *jardin clos*, itself a symbol of the Virgin's immaculate conception, hence the Madonna is often shown in, or in front of an enclosed garden. This was usually only a few paces square and is grassed, not paved, and surrounded with wattle fences or low walls, which recalled in miniature the crenellated ramparts of the castle but probably were put up as a protection against wandering pigs and poultry rather than marauders. In an era of lawlessness the walled garden reflected the same need for security felt by the town, but replaced its battlements and turrets with walls of greenery. The hedges of clipped bay were sometimes mixed with lentiscus, myrtle was festooned with honeysuckle and bushes of broom·or bay grew in stone or terracotta pots, box-edged parterres were filled with flowers, the wall covered with roses, wisteria, ivy or jessamine and a gentle trickling fountain completed the picture of peaceful ease.

If the garden was fairly large it was often divided into two parts, one the small enclosure already described, the other an area dedicated to herbs and a *bosco*, or place for cooking, in fact a barbecue. The illustrations of many illuminated manuscripts and Books of Hours show small gardens of this description which give excellent ideas for similarly sized modern gardens. Often the seats are not of stone but of turf built up around a tree-trunk or along a wall, closely bound with wattle and surfaced with grass. It is odd that this attractive item is rarely seen today, though a contemporary version was created by Vita Sackville-West in her garden at Sissinghurst where a flat seat in the herb garden was cushioned by thyme, not grass.

With the coming of humanism in Europe the respective rôles of art and religion parted, mythology replaced the Bible stories and the 'Mary gardens' became the secular *giardinos segretos* of the Renaissance. Most of these followed the same pattern as the medieval walled garden and there are many examples to be seen in pictures of the time. In the *Annunciation* by Domenico Veneziano one corner shows two columns on either side of an ivy-covered archway leading to a tiny rose garden through a door with a huge lock on it, the partitions between the two gardens composed of canes covered with roses.

The raised beds which are a feature of many classical and medieval gardens also deserve greater attention than they receive nowadays. The reason for their origin is manifest; the insignificant flowers of long-ago, the violets, daisies and small iris (*Iris germanica*) native to Western Europe needed to be seen at close quarters; trailing plants such as periwinkles and ivy could grow and hang over the edges which were easy to see, and no stooping was required, surely as much a convenience then as now.

One of the most perfect *giardinos segretos* ever conceived was that of Isabella Gonzaga's in the palace of Mantua. The tiny apartments to which Isabella d'Este retired after her widow-

The importance of adequately framing a doorway is exquisitely portrayed in this detail of an Annunciation by D. Veneziano where a simple stone arch leads to a short paved walk and a flower framed, firmly barred wooden door. 43

A small pavilion at the far end of Mrs. Anthony Crossley's Chelsea garden makes a wind-shielded sun-trap but also doubles as a tool and potting shed to which access is obtained by the rear door in the centre.

hood are as superb as they are small. Inevitably they include the pleasure of a garden and the magnificent intarsia walls and golden ceilings of the salon look on to a court enriched by columns and statues. Fig and apple trees and jasmines once added perfume and living beauty but though they have vanished the small enclosure still strikes the onlooker as a miniature paradise.

In the same vast palace is another garden room, thought by Georgina Masson to be the most beautiful of all. The little Giardino Pensile, so-called because it was built on a level with the piano nobile, is enclosed on three sides by loggias supported by exquisitely carved columns, which give it a cloistered air. A somewhat similar garden room in the Roman Palazzo Venezia was built a century earlier than the Mantovan example— perhaps in design too shady for modern sun-lovers but which deserves to be studied by those who seek shelter and seclusion.

Outdoor rooms have always been part of the Italian way of life—what is a piazza but the unroofed family room of the whole city? In the fifteenth century Leone Battista Alberti, who may

44

be said to be the first to state the principles of modern gardening, suggested a startling variant to the usual rectangular
plan and recommended a semi-circular shape for the garden
walls, asserting it would provide the maximum shelter from
winds. Parkinson did not agree with him and considered a
square form the best shape since all the windows of the house
could look on it comfortably—a tenet which still holds good in
our rows of terraced town houses.

In Tuscany these *giardinos segretos* became a great feature
of country villas and, as they could be entered only through the
apartments of the owner, they were truly secret from all except
a few dozen visitors and their suggestion of the hidden and unexpected undoubtedly gave a special sense of enjoyment to
those permitted to share their delights. They were often decorated with paintings of fountains, birds and plants as well as
real flowers and when the pleasures of reading novels grew more
popular, became the venue of many informal gatherings. It
must have been in such surroundings that the lucky few who
had escaped from pest-ridden Florence to the healthy peace of
the country-side first heard the tales read by Boccaccio who
wrote that his listeners sat on grass of the deepest green starred
with a thousand flowers.

Many of these gardens contained small loggias which were
constructed with careful attention to the style of the main
building and sited so that they were open to the sun but gave
protection from the wind.

The furnishings of a garden-room, nearly always of stone or
marble, were sometimes composed of tiles in the Iberian penin-
sula. The beautifully patterned seats of the Alcazar gardens,
or the fantastic tiled garden in Lumiar near Lisbon have no
counterparts in the north but the Chinese porcelain seats,
charming but uncomfortable, are often seen in sheltered gardens
though now, alas, hard to find and high in price. Apart from
the necessary table and seats most garden rooms included a
number of large pots in which sweet-smelling herbs could be
planted. Madame de Stael, discussing outdoor rooms, suggested
an Aeolian harp should be hung nearby so that the pleasures
of sound could be added to that of fragrance—both amenities
which could be included in the smallest town back-garden. She
could not foresee the ubiquitous, all-pervading radio.

Another exceptionally successful loggia is that of San Martino
at Palma, praised by Bernard Berenson as one of the few spots
on earth where art and nature were felt to be in perfect harmony. He described it as a 'rustic Parthenon' so much did he

The garden seats of Lumiar have high curved backs and, like the walls, are composed of tiles, chiefly in shades of aubergine purple, blue, yellow and white. Most of these depict rural scenes or views of boats on canals.

admire the proportions of the stone and wood construction, and though not many garden rooms can hope to gain equally high praise those who wish to build a loggia would do well to look carefully at its measurements and the spacing of its columns.

A modern equivalent might take the form of a garden pavilion along one wall with two windows and a centre opening, the interior furnished by stone seats and a table so that meals can be taken without the palaver (and horrible appearance) of movable garden furniture. To-day's foam cushions add a comfort to stone unknown to our hardier ancestors. It is a good idea to arrange the furnishings as similar as possible to an indoor room, with chairs and table conveniently placed for conversation, and to use pots with plants in lieu of vases with flowers. A famous example which carries this idea to excess is the Hermitage garden room in Bayreuth where a low fence

46

No garden goes farther in the elimination of nature than that of Lumiar, near Lisbon, where the only plants are those in a series of handsome urns set on a balustrade which, like the walls, seats and columns, are all composed of decorative tiles portraying country views, trees and pavilions.

Another view of the Lumiar tiled garden which dates from the eighteenth century shows pictures of the exotic birds then recently brought from South America and Africa, strange toucans, ostriches, parakeets and turkeys, all set in a baroque frame.

and gate is painted on the walls, in one corner is a fire-place and the roof is sky blue.

In most urban areas there is no lack of water and a fountain is not a necessity but is always a delight, a small spray or a mere drip of water from a great shell or ornamental lead spout can give unending pleasure. It is simple to install a small pump operated from the mains for around six or seven pounds.

Nowhere is water a more important item than in the patio.

This term, now often used incorrectly, refers to an open central area entirely surrounded by the house in the same manner as the atrium of a classical building, a concept brought by the Moors to Spain where it is the core of family life. Small courtyards, glimpsed through iron grilles set in sombre door-ways, are one of the great charms of Spanish towns, especially in Cordova where a week, or a month, can be passed wandering through its white-washed streets looking at the pictures formed by a fountain or centre pool surrounded by green plants and brilliantly coloured flowers in pots. The famous Casa de

A garden used for open-air eating is given a semblance of shelter and roofing by a judicious use of wooden slats. Planting is kept to the minimum and a creeper covered wall, a narrow bed and some shrubs make a really labour-free courtyard.

Pilatos in Seville, so-called because it is said to be a copy of Pilate's house in Jerusalem, has its area divided into separate compartments by rectangular stone paths edged with low borders of clipped lavender or box and shrubs in huge Ali Baba jars.

Pots and jars are an excellent means of furnishing the out-door room. Originally made as storage jars for oil, wine and grain they only later appeared in the garden but some evidence that they definitely had been used as flower-pots came to light when the foundations of the Athenian Agora were excavated and reconstructed in the late Thirties. Herbs and small shrubs were grown in pots in most medieval gardens and many illuminated manuscripts show pots perched on castle walls or placed in the small, enclosed gardens. Later, when fortified buildings gave way to wide terraces and open vistas, pots continued to be part of the garden furnishings. The Dutch garden, introduced into England at the time when William of Orange came to the throne, used pots extensively but preferred them of stone

49

or lead rather than earthenware. Pots remained much in evidence until the landscape school ousted the formal garden and caused their disappearance. During the Victorian era some large and heavy terracotta pots were made, chiefly by firms concerned with the new sanitary fitments, and late in the century Mrs. G. F. Watts founded the Potter's Art Guild in an attempt to revive this ancient craft.

Although a number of pots are made in this country they are predominantly a product of sunnier climes where the soil is thin and rocky and water in short supply. The Mediterranean littoral has long been known for its oil jars, Spain and Portugal with their strong Moorish influence use many in their patios, Italy, particularly Florence, is famous for its pots, and in recent years the ancient pottery at Vaullauris in the Alpes Maritimes, which dates back to Roman times, was revived by Picasso.

Now the advantages of pots for growing plants are being noted by the town gardener who can then control the soil and give each plant its correct nourishment. Furthermore weeding is made easy and the pot has the advantage of allowing it to be turned around so the plant receives equal light on all sides. It should be remembered that most pots are of earthenware which is slightly porous and, as a certain amount of evaporation takes place, watering must be carefully watched. Pots should never be placed on grass but always stand on stone or brick.

Although pots can be of many shapes they have retained a remarkable similarity of style throughout thousands of years. The great storage jars in the Minoan palace at Knossos, the Chinese butter jars of 3,000 B.C. such as the one in the garden at Sissinghurst, the shapely oil jars made in classical times, the plain flower-pots or their decorative variants with fluted edges or raised bands, the Moorish long-handled jars with pointed ends (to facilitate burying in the sand though now seen supported by wrought iron stands) are still cast in many countries. In all this wide variety there is hardly a shape which is not a joy to look at.

The same cannot be said of surface, and the violently coloured glazes of the flower pots which decorate the walls and gardens in Southern Europe are among the more deplorable etceteras of the modern home. Garish colours, which inevitably clash with each other and with the plants which fill them, should be avoided, but some of the plain glazes in dark green, grey and brown are delightful and glazing or painting with a hard gloss

The increased use of glass in the Twenties altered the concept of the house and garden dichotomy. The outdoors invaded the house and the room expanded outward. One wall of this sitting-room opens to unite room and garden.

The luxury of one tree is permitted in a severe plan of the Thirties where bentwood chairs in the fashionable Breuer-Bauhaus style stand on square stone paving and metal rods support a light canopy.

helps to prevent evaporation. The decorative blue and white glazed vases, such as those which stand in the gardens of the pavilion-palace of Queluz, are more difficult to incorporate in a northern garden but can be extremely effective. However, they might not withstand a severe winter and would need protection by sacking or polythene sheets, thus creating unsightly objects to be avoided in a small garden where the entire area is immediately visible. The large pots once used for lemon and orange trees, usually decorated with moulded swags, are excellent for a rather sophisticated garden and provide ample space for a small rhododendron or a camellia. Large strawberry-pots with apertures in their sides offer good breeding grounds for small rock pinks, *Aubretias*, *alyssums* and miniature phlox—or even for the strawberries for which the delightful shape was originally devised.

Trailing plants look particularly well in pots with narrow necks, *Campanula isophylla* is a lovely choice, ivyleafed geraniums a summer best, fuchsias and lobelias a happy mixture, and the small variegated ivy a good contrast to a green-glazed jar. Pots with a wide neck are best planted with upright shrubs, preferably evergreens. *Elaeagnus pungens maculata* with its gold-splashed green and white leaves is a good all-the-year attraction. A wide-necked jar offers the opportunity of planting a few miniature bulbs, snowdrops, grape-hyacinths or scyllas, around the base of the plant for an early spring display.

A type of pot rarely seen in this country is the wall-pot familiar to all who know Spain where some of the small towns show whitewashed houses gay with brilliant geraniums growing in pots attached to the walls by iron rings. This device offers a simple method of adding summer colour to a garden-room where climbers either are not required or are not yet grown sufficiently to clothe the walls. If possible it is a good idea to use a double pot, one inside the other, in order to prevent undue evaporation. So far the lure of imitation rockwork pots does not seem to have reached contemporary collectors, though undoubtedly the fashion will return in due course, but the cast-iron or wire pots, fancy baskets and flower stands made in the latter part of the last century are now keenly sought after by modern gardeners.

One of the best uses to which pots can be put is for growing herbs. So many are of a spreading habit that it is better to restrict them and to grow each type in a separate container and so give each plant its preferred soil and situation. Nothing is more refreshing or rewarding for the town gardener than to be able to cut herbs for the cooking pot or salad bowl fresh from his own plants, so incomparably better than the dried varieties, most of which taste like stale hay. Most herbs grow best in a compost enriched with rotted manure, bone-meal, with an occasional dose of plant food. For basil, chervil, sorrel and mint good drainage and full sun are important, rosemary likes a dry soil and some shelter from North East winds. Chives and mint should be kept damp, parsley, which should be renewed annually, likes a rich soil.

Some herbs are as decorative as they are useful, sage, either the variegated form with crimson, white and mauve leaves, or the lovely *Salvia officinalis Tricolor* is always colourful; the upright brush of Sweet Marjoram has white flowers and the glossy green and purple foliage of basil is always attractive. Tarragon is a rather thin, straggly plant but so important for the kitchen that it must be included, but be sure to acquire the French, not the Russian, variety, and give it a well-tilled soil with plenty of humus and good drainage as otherwise the roots

A dank and dreary backyard surrounded with high walls was transformed into an enchanted grotto by the ingenuity of Kenneth Villiers. He paved the entire area, creating different levels, placed columns on either side of a classical statue, made a feature of a weeping wych elm that, with yuccas, ferns and hostas, is floodlit at night.

will rot. In a largish pot it could be given a 'collar' of parsley so that the latter's rich green curls conceal its leggy growth.

The garden room, like the courtyard, requires uniform ground surface and the idiosyncrasies of crazy paving is too rustic and untidy for what should aim to be a room without a roof. A design which recalls a carpet or rug would be appropriate, a pattern of square slabs surrounded by an edge of bricks, or rectangular stones interspersed with brick units bordered by plain stone, or alternate plain and pebble-set cement squares with a stone border. Many varieties can be composed of units of two, three or four bricks laid in different ways to form the centre of the 'carpet', with a border of straight horizontal bricks.

A creeper surrounding a false door in the far wall can give an air of mystery and suggest unexplored possibilities. Tubs with clipped box or bay trees will give a rich background and still permit an under-planting of scyllas for a breath of spring or white hanging campanulas for summer beauty. A few hydrangeas planted in semi-circular corner beds and some reliable spring flowering bulbs, such as mauve and white crocuses (not the yellow which the birds destroy), and Kaufmannia tulips or hyacinths which will flower three months before the hydrangeas begin to leaf and need not be dug up each year. Some late miniature dahlias might be added to give colour until autumn puts paid to such ephemeral delights and leaves only the sombre richness of green.

Columns are put to dramatic effect on the terrace of a Louisiana plantation house, painted by Felix Kelly. On it stands a bentwood rocker, until recently a relic of Victorian days, now once more the height of fashion.

ENTRANCES AND PATHWAYS

A detail woefully neglected in most urban gardens is the means of access which more often resembles anonymous rabbit-holes than an important part of a human habitation. The emphasis placed on doorways in the East, and in those western countries which were influenced by the baroque taste, is wholly lacking in most modern building schemes, some of which appear to hide the entrance as if it were a shameful necessity. The Hayward Gallery in London—where even the knowledgeable taxi drivers find difficulty in depositing their fares at the right place—is an outstanding example of this way of thinking.

Europe has never paid the extreme attention to the doorway that it commands in the Orient where the arch symbolises the entrance to Paradise. The immense doorways of Persia, often leading to very little, the magnificent entrances to small pavilions, gardens and *caravanserais* have never had their counterpart even in the most palatial architecture in the West. The ubiquitous European rectilinear form is only one of many shapes seen in the Far East; Chinese garden entrances are often circular, octagonal or leaf-shaped but are never sited opposite each other as this might facilitate the passage of evil spirits.

The columned and pedimented archways of the classical era, the baroque entrances of seventeenth century palaces, the elaborate iron-work of later days are not compatible with the modest demands of today but the small scale of contemporary gardens makes careful attention to detail all the more important.

The most obvious example in the West of the Eastern attention to the doorway is to be seen in the architecture of Moorish Spain where splendid doorways are a feature of urban architecture and the superb arches of the Alhambra are echoed in miniature in every side street. In medieval times there were still memories of the arch as a symbol of the entrance to eternal life and the arch is an important item on many descriptions and illustration of early gardens and these, considerably less ambitious than their Oriental contemporaries, offer many suggestions for the small garden of today. The symbolism of the arch has been forgotten but the beauty of its shape still pleases.

Later ages developed iron-work as a peep-show to the paradise garden within and the art of the iron-worker became a major attraction of many of the great gardens throughout Europe. Much emphasis was placed on the element of surprise when, through an iron-work door, an arch or a trellis, a view of the garden could be glimpsed. The splendid tradition of English ironwork diminished in the nineteenth century, but as the growth of large building developments near towns coincided with new techniques in the manufacture of wrought iron, what had been a rich man's privilege came within the means of the well-to-do citizens.

The work of Thomas Jeckyll, so much admired in his day, ignored or despised by the last generation and now once more returning to favour, was typical of the aesthetic of his day, but the inevitable change in taste took place and neither Lutyens nor Gertrude Jekyll favoured such elaborate designs in close association with nature.

Lutyens, with the restraint typical of his style, composed simple but effective entrances and strove to restore the lost status of the garden door. One of his favourite signatures was a wooden door with a rounded top emphasized by splayed bricks and a stone coping set in a brick wall: a particularly interesting example was composed of red roofing tiles arranged in semi-circular rays, topped with several layers of coping stones,

In a small space it is often a good idea to construct steps in a semi-circular shape like these wooden ones, held together by iron staples, at the entrance of a fifteenth-century country house.

57

another offered an entrance through a brick arch filled with a fine, but simple, ironwork door. Such an entrance can also be the excuse to build a small overhanging porch useful both as a protection from the weather and as a support for a climber. A pair of plant-filled pots on either side of such a doorway can do much to reduce a doleful back entrance. In creating such effects the main consideration obviously must be the proportions and style of the house: if it is built in a neo-georgian idiom the addition of two half-columns and a plain pediment to the doorway is the obvious and perhaps the most successful choice, but with more contemporary architecture another and less conventional style is required. A smooth-surfaced door, well proportioned, with individually designed furniture of knocker and handle would be suitable.

The pace of urban development has allowed little thought and less scope for these refinements, and the access of most town gardens is rendered difficult by sharp, ungainly steps and paths too narrow for comfort or elegance. If there is sufficient space and a difference of level two or three narrow treads can be widened into a semi-circular shape either of stone or splayed bricks, a decorative and practical method often seen in medieval house-and-garden pictures which became popular again early in this century. The raised bank formed on either side of such steps is an ideal situation for growing rock plants. Good combinations are the early flowering mauve and lavender aubretias with the silvery foliaged *Alyssum saxatile*, blue aubretias with the yellow of *Alyssum saxatile citrinus*, and with rose-coloured helianthemums. Dwarf campanulas, particularly the trailing *Campanula garganica* are lovely with the bright pinks of *Dianthus caesius* and *Dianthus deltoides*. The purple-blue *Viola cornuta* will flourish in the shade but the crimson *Saxifraga bathoniensis* needs sun, so does the tangerine *Geum Borisii* and *Lithospermum* Heavenly Blue. All these early summer flowers can be preceded by the miniature daffodils, no more than three or four inches high, snowdrops, scyllas and primulas, and these tiny flowers are an especial delight when they can be seen almost at eye-level.

The placing of a window or of an opening in the wall in order to frame a view is seldom seen in town gardens for the good reason there is seldom anything pleasant to emphasize,

The circular motif of this tiny garden is repeated in shallow curved steps which lead from a paved to a pebbled area. The steps, like the retaining border of the flower beds, are of brick, giving variety of texture to a strictly limited design.   59

but if there is an opportunity to set off a near-by shrub by this method it should not be missed. An excellent example can be seen in a garden near Henley, said to have been laid out by Evelyn, where oval apertures at intervals in a high dividing wall frame entrancing pictures of flower beds on the other side. If, in more modest surroundings, a carefully placed *oeil de boeuf* could reveal a neighbour's plant or a pleasant vista down a tree-lined street a new interest could be created.

The fashion of covering a garden door with mirror-glass to give an additional view, so popular some years ago, has been revived recently with great success in a heavily over-shadowed London garden where it is given interest by a Gothic window filled with mirror set into the wall facing the house. The glancing light of the glass, romantically framed by plants and creepers, reflects back the garden's centre-piece of a stone wellhead surrounded by camellias in winter and geraniums in summer.

A path always should be a pleasure, either an immediate convenience or a suggestion of as yet unknown delights, preferably both. Paths were part of the amenities of the gardens built in the outskirts of Rome in the time of the Caesars when every household of any standing had its *ambulatio* with the ground prepared with the utmost care so that it should be plastic and soft to the foot, but not disintegrate into a sea of mud when it rained. Vitruvius' description of how carefully the alleys were laid down sounds very like the preparations made for our modern tennis courts and the excellence of their walks was a status symbol whereby the wealth of the owners could be gauged. The poor had uneven, uncomfortable stones, the wealthy smooth well-prepared paths.

The ground plan of most medieval gardens was usually that in which Paradise itself was represented: a walled square with four paths and in the centre a fountain symbolising the waters of life, a design which persisted with variations for centuries until balanced symmetry was supplanted by the curves of the landscape school. An alternative to the usual square was the presentation of paradise as a circle, a pattern rarely followed in private gardens but which was the shape of the first great botanical garden in Europe, built in Padua in 1545. This comprises a perfect circle of eighty-four metres subdivided into sixteen equal divisions, again subdivided until each small bed

A mirror-filled Gothic window in a bleak back wall gives extra light and reflects an urn filled and surrounded with gay geraniums.

The allegories beloved by the Middle Ages credited this tiny garden with a naked Venus and two fashionably dressed ladies, Juno and Pallas. Paths divide the grass into even squares and a narrow bed of flowers runs beside the crenellated walls. Emilia's Garden, Bibliothèque Nationale, Paris.

contains one species or genus. At the end of one of the paths still stands the small greenhouse where stood the palm which inspired Goethe to write the *Metamorphosis of Plants*.

The circular garden has had few descendants but the plan of four corner plots, four paths and a fountain or well-head in the centre is still one of the most satisfactory for a small square particularly if the beds are planted with roses and edged with pinks, or the more easily grown Heuchera. Care must be taken that all the roses are of the same height in all four beds, and that each bed contains only one species. The pure white of Iceberg would contrast well with the velvety red of Lili Marlene, or the blush pink and white of Picasso with the clear yellow of

62

The gardens of Renaissance Italy often showed terraces and paths of beautifully arranged marbles in contrasting colours, a refinement rarely acceptable in the damp North, but it is often possible to achieve an interesting pattern by a juxtaposition brick and stone. Giovanni Bellini, detail from Allegory of the Tree of Life, Uffizi.

Jan Spek. A completely new idiom was derived from the expressionist movement in art soon after the First World War, best illustrated in the house built by Walter Gropius, in collaboration with Adolf Meyer, in 1920 at Berlin-Zehlendorf West. Here manneristic devices were applied to both house and garden, the entrance to the courtyard was on diagonal lines and the house placed on an axial plan with the garden laid out in paved zig-zag walks and flower beds at acute angles transfixed by a straight path. This was geometry as Lutyens did not know it, yet it somewhat recalled the 'butterfly' design of houses beloved by the advanced Edwardian architect, E. S. Prior, of which Home Place, High Kelling near Norwich, built in 1903, is an example.

Few items of garden construction are more agreeable to the eye than a well-laid and well-raked path of small, even gravel which contrasts so well with the green of a lawn or the grey of a stone-edged pool or seat. Gravel paths have been a feature

An ingenious combination of uneven stones and two different bituminous surfaces is bordered and outlined in brick in an unusual curved pattern.

of English gardens since the seventeenth century and Pepys maintained that English gravel walks were the best in the world, and that neither France nor Italy had any to compare. Nevertheless gravel paths combed in careful swirls, similar to the Marcel waves of a pre-1914 *coiffure*, still can be found in old-fashioned Italian country resorts but are rarely seen, and even more rarely admired in this country.

To maintain over a large area a well-distributed gravel surface imposes a certain amount of work, but a relatively narrow path is not difficult. The advice given in the fifteenth century by Alberti on the planning of garden paths still holds good and nothing looks more satisfactory than an edging of clipped box. It should also be remembered that such a miniature hedge also plays an important rôle in protecting seedlings from winds and in aerating the air around them. Alternatively, Alberti suggested scented evergreens such as the low-growing light grey *artemisia stelleriana* which can be cut back to four

64

inches and looks well with the tawny colour of the gravel pebbles but is too similar in shade to form a sufficient contrast to stone against which a pale *hosta* or the miniature Hidcote lavender looks well.

In France the humble brown pebble is often replaced by glittering white chips which make an excellent foil for the dark green of box but have an undeniable air of sophistication. This makes them good companions to a scheme of elaborate trellis work and formal bedding-out, but are not advisable if a simpler, less pretentious effect is desired.

Paths entirely composed of concrete should be avoided for they crack and soon look sordid but if blocks of concrete are alternated with squares of grass, or thin lines of grass are used to outline each concrete square a reasonably attractive effect can be achieved. Paths of narrow concrete squares with borders of pebbles on either side is a good choice, so is a chequer-board of alternate squares of pebbles and concrete blocks. Pre-fabricated concrete slabs mixed with pebbles can be obtained

A non-slip studded concrete floor is given an over-all interest by the superimposition of a shadow diamond pattern, left.
A rough but attractive surface can be achieved by a mixture of bitumen and stone chips which ensures a firm foothold and offers a pleasing scheme of shaded tones of grey, right.

in several geometric variations including some similar to the pebble diamond and star design to be seen in the Boboli gardens and all of these are improved by a brick surround. Concrete slabs must be laid on an even surface of at least two inches of builders' sand, or on rubble and held by five spots of a lime and mortar mixture, with narrow gaps between each so that water can drain away and the path remain dry. Slabs suitable for such a purpose can be obtained in a variety of colours, with a non-slip surface, which is a boon both for the very young and very old. Great care must be exercised if it is decided to use more than one colour and a mixture can result in an unfortunate bathroom floor effect. It is safer to stick to the natural tones of pebble grey.

Most bricks are pleasant in colour and have the advantage of drying quickly. The patterns in which they can be arranged are legion, the most popular is the square composed of two pairs laid alternately horizontally and vertically, or with the bricks placed with their points at an acute angle to form a zig-zag or chevrons. Most paths in the early Dutch gardens were entirely of bricks as are, or were, the paths of cottage gardens all over England.

Paths of York stone are the most practical and the easiest to maintain, but are also expensive, though less costly if all the stones are not of the same size and shape. A happy compromise between formality and *laissez-faire* is achieved by the paved walk in the beech-grove at Sissinghurst where rectangles of different sizes are arranged to form a wide path in which some small rock plants bloom in the odd crevices. If the stones are broken up and a so-called crazy pavement is created from the pieces it is a good plan to plant sweet-scented thyme in the cracks and small uneven spaces. Paths of granite paving-block stone are always agreeable, and paths of separate stones leading through a lawn to a door in a wall, even if the latter leads to no more than the potting shed which Kipling called 'the heart of it all' but was given a far different definition by Grahame Greene.

A grass path is always a joy to look at though perhaps not always the best choice in a damp climate. Nothing gives a more restful air than an *ambulatio*, a green path close to a low stone wall, with perhaps small, low-growing plants such as violets, *Iris unguicularis*, crocus and hart's-tongue ferns growing in a narrow bed at its base. A short green walk is a splendid foil to dark surroundings and the trouble of moving and rolling well worth while in order to achieve an air of cloistered peace. One very small garden in modern Amsterdam, a mere square overshadowed by big trees, had a narrow carpet of grass around a central urn filled with bright geraniums which gave a delightful duet of green and red.

Tiled paths are suitable for a garden laid out in a very formal manner, but a tessellated path usually has a rather institutional air and the lovely pavements and paths composed of differently coloured marble, so exquisitely illustrated in many Italian Renaissance paintings, are not practical in the cold and damp of the North. A pleasingly country air can be achieved if an old mill-stone can be found to give importance to the end of a path or a doorstep surrounded with bricks and a border of flagstones.

For centuries the only acceptable path was the straight path. It appears in the earliest known gardens, such as those depicted on Egyptian frescoes where the design was imposed by the irrigation canals essential to the survival of the garden. This pattern remained the only acceptable one for many centuries: the peristyle of Roman houses, the small enclosures glimpsed in medieval manuscripts, the Renaissance gardens of Italy and Holland and the great European gardens of the eighteenth century all show straight paths until the arrival of the landscape school. The turning and winding paths which then superseded the stiff geometric lay-outs became popular in England as early as the beginning of the eighteenth century when one aesthete went as far as to ask "is there anything more ridiculous and forbidding, than a garden which is regular?"

The mutations of taste are incalculable; Defoe wrote admiringly of a straight walk at Hampton Court bounded by tall clipped hedges, but only a few years later a critic remarked of this same avenue that "to every person of taste it must be very far from affording any pleasure". He assumed that every discriminating person was a convert to the new landscape school which abhorred a straight line, whereas Defoe echoed the beliefs of such Renaissance theorists as Leone Battista Alberti who sought order everywhere and recommended symmetrical proportions, a concept in its turn derived from the teaching of Vitruvius. The romantic school abolished straight rows of trees "answering to one another" and replaced them by planting designed to emulate the careless bounty of nature. The neo-classical architects strove to cleanse design from the wanton freaks of the rococo—but fashions come and go in gardens, just as they do in music or the height of skirt hems. Some flowers become nearly extinct for lack of a fashionable

An interesting essay in free-hand design can be seen in the terrace of a house in Helsinki, designed by Alvar Aalto, where order has been conjured out of the apparently chaotic materials of irregularly shaped stones and earth.

interest in them, and the Royal Horticultural Society post-bag is full of queries and laments about fast vanishing old-fashioned flowers.

By the time the Romatic era dawned in literature and the arts there was hardly a straight path to be found in the garden of any gentleman's residence. Only the proletariat continued to favour a straight line from gate to door, and from back-door to vegetable plot. When the second Earl Harcourt, a fervent disciple of J. J. Rousseau, entrusted the design of his garden to the poet William Mason, he requested "romantic glades suitable for noble savages." The poet re-created what he imagined to be Julie's 'natural' garden with winding paths and irregu-

68

Another Northern example of the use of rough stones is in the Carl Milles garden at Tillhör where they give a rich pattern to the supporting walls of a steeply winding path.

larly shaped flower beds, the 'wavy line of beauty' was everywhere, and the English blue-stocking Elizabeth Montague said that it "excelled every flower garden which ever existed either in history or romance"—nevertheless it might have seemed faintly unfamiliar to any visiting 'noble savage'. The so-called *jardin Anglais* was copied all over Europe and Voltaire's garden Les Delices in Switzerland was laid out in the English style. Humphrey Repton, one of the leaders of the romantic landscape school, proclaimed that meaning must be given to every curve by the careful planting of trees and that no paths should be straight that could curve. The Empress Josephine was of the same opinion and permitted no straight paths at Malmaison.

69

Repton advised that when a path or walk led to some particular objective, such as a fountain, statue or seat, it should return by another route so that the *promeneur* was not forced to turn back on his tracks. He also pointed out that when two walks meet they should do so at right angles in order not to leave an awkward point. Such refinements are not often feasible in small areas but it is sometimes more satisfactory to place a special point of interest in one corner rather than in the centre of a wall and so allow the path to encircle the total area of the garden rather than become a mere walk to and from house and object. One exceptionally successful London garden has transformed the usual oblong shape by an oval lawn surrounded by a stone path with triangular beds filling in the angles.

Another has allowed the path at the far end to merge into a paved area large enough to accommodate a gazebo on either side of which are corner beds raised a foot from the ground by a border of bricks. Yet another method of varying the contour of the path can be obtained by arranging tile boxes of identical size and shape to form a series of recessed patterns, thus narrowing the path and widening the beds as the path recedes from the house. A long oblong garden which has kept its original shape but attained a most successful effect has a small semi-circular paved court near the house, with urns standing sentinel at the entrance to a long path winding down to a heavy clump of trees, beneath which are a seat in one corner and a statue in the other. The flower beds on either side of the path are backed by large shrubs with clumps of lower-growing plants in front spilling into uneven shapes in order to break up its straight line. But this treatment would not be the success it is without the dense shade of the trees at the end, which give an air of mystery to a very humdrum layout.

It is noteworthy that most of the gardens which received popular acclaim and carried off the prizes at both the *Daily Mail* and *Daily Express* competitions at the Chelsea Flower Show in 1970 favoured unsymmetrical designs with winding paths. The classic rectangle appears to have disappeared in England but to have found a new and interesting expression in the New World. The stiff rectangular lines of the splendid garden at the Museum of Modern Art in Rio de Janeiro, designed by Burle Marx, echoes in unusually successful contemporary terms the Roman love of symmetry.

Garden fashions resemble those of dress in their international scope and swiftly changing tastes, and a common market in garden design and plant breeding has existed in Europe since the days of the Roman Empire. Chief among cosmopolitan garden figures are three generations of the Mollet family who served the English and Swedish courts as well as the French, bringing with them the taste and knowledge gained from other countries. The eldest Mollet is reputed to have been the originator of the *broderies* so much appreciated in the seventeenth, and so much derided in the nineteenth, century and is certainly responsible for the 'typically French' *patte d'oie* and the radiating straight rides at the head of Hampton Court's large canal.

Few people today would wish to construct such paths as an Egyptian pasha caused to be made in a pleasure ground created for a beloved wife which were composed of a mosaic in bright curlicues in red, yellow and black. Nor do the walks in the Güell Park in Barcelona, the work of that incredible fantasist Gaudi, in many-coloured mosaic depicting strange animals, appeal to many, but some, surely, would like to emulate the lovely paths of *pietra compressa* or crushed shells which are a feature of many Italian gardens.

Easier to create, though rarely attempted, are paths of pebbles, seen at their best at the Villa Caprarola, which are commonplace around the Mediterranean but rare in the North. Paths in elaborate designs carried out in differently shaded and sized pebbles are to be found in sea-side villages from the Black Sea to the Atlantic shores of Portugal. The Greek islands favour scrolls, leaves and birds, the more geometric Spanish designs show the influence of the Moors, and the Portuguese abstract swirling patterns composed of light and dark grey pebbles are endlessly delightful to look at if hard on the feet. To watch Spanish workmen in a garden at Granada planning and placing the correct pebbles on a bed of sand before setting them firmly in concrete, taking care that they had found the exact size and gradation of colour required, is to see craftsmen employing their talents to their fullest extent, not workmen doing a dull task. This age-old craft has crossed the Atlantic and has developed in the South American cities where the glittering modernity of their buildings is set off by pavements in dramatic black and white abstract designs, curiously similar in their diminishing perspective to the paintings of Brigit Riley and Vasarely but which antedate both these artists by several decades.

It is a thousand pities that this delightful craft of pebble-mosaic is not encouraged in small backyards where it would give interest and a sense of richness on the dullest day. The collecting of pebbles would be a fine summer holiday task, and that of setting them in a patterned path an excellent job for autumn days when the season for gardening is over.

When laying out a path it is a good rule to make it wider than is necessary, nothing is more niggling and uncomfortable for walking than a meanly narrow path. Two comfortably abreast, with the possibility of a third, must be the minimum. In the small, walled gardens the Dutch of the seventeenth century allowed a generous space for the paths which helped to create a feeling of space and luxury. An exception is when an air of mystery is required when a narrow path winding into the distance can look inviting, but this is a quality not often called for in town gardens.

One of the most intriguing uses to which the path can be put is to create an illusion of distance. A small area can be made to appear far larger than it is if down its centre runs a wide path which diminishes in width as it recedes from the house. A path of five feet wide can in thirty or so yards diminish to one foot, and this illusion of depth and space can be increased if a proportionately small gate or small statue is placed at its far end on a slightly higher level. There are many manuals which give the rules of perspective but Dr. Brook Taylor's *Method of Perspective Made Easy* published in 1754 is still good reading.

The carefully scaled size of the chosen stonework or sculpture has much to do with the felicity of effect. An excellent example of this trick is in the Palazzo Podesta in Genoa where the juxtaposition of a small statue to a restricted area appears to increase its size. Another, in a very different context, is a contemporary English country garden where a narrow path on a gradual upward slope ends with a small statue which, by the careful use of perspective and the diminishing height of the bordering shrubs, is made to appear as if far-away in a (comparatively) large park.

The contrast between these two small (or far-away) objects can be accentuated if two large pots with plants are placed at the beginning of the path near the house, and fairly large trees grown at the far garden wall with small statues on either side of an opening thus creating the impression of a long path leading to a wood—a charming conceit for an urban area.

Another and most successful method of giving an appearance of space is to make a path, diminishing in width, curve abruptly behind a group of shrubs or a small summer house, which gives an illusionist trick of apparent distance. A particularly successful garden in South Kensington, a few hundred yards from the underground station, has achieved an air of park-like space in a mere half acre by such clever planning.

A path, sharply diminishing in width, disappears behind a bosky corner where trees are reflected in a shallow pool, suggesting a walk into a wood. If we are to agree with Edmund Burke that "no work of Art can be great but as it deceives" then this suburban garden can properly be included in the realm of art. In any case it is an unusual idea to follow when making a garden.

In a shady corner of her South Kensington garden Primrose Harley sketched a flower-filled urn with a hosta on one side.

THE TRELLIS

The trellis is a valuable item of town gardening which has a past as delightful as its appearance. Its name derives from *treillage* or vine tendrils, and the construction somehow manages to retain all the charm of its origin while being as useful as it is decorative. It appears in some of the earliest gardens recorded: Egyptian frescoes show rounded arbours roofed with grape-hung vines, and a luxuriant trellis covers the painted ceiling of the XVIII Dynasty Gardener's tomb, one of the first gardeners known to history. Roman Livia's garden-room had a trellis painted round it, Sallust's garden at Pompeii had a pergola covered by a vine, and many of the gardens glimpsed in illuminated manuscripts show a trellis surrounding their small enclosures. In several illustrations in the *Roman de la Rose* green galleries support climbing plants and separate one section of the garden from another. The Persians too loved an open bower and built many surrounded with low trellis walls but nearly always approached by imposing doorways which were always an important item in Persian architecture.

The trellis appears in innumerable paintings of the early Renaissance: Cima de Conegliane's *Madonna with James and Jerome* shows an arched vine-covered trellis; a similar one

A high trellis smothered in roses shelters an enchanted garden in which stands the fountain of love and some of its devotees. Accredited to Antonio Vivarini's studio, now in the National Gallery, Melbourne, Australia.

forms the shade-giving roof to the house in the background of Antonello de Messina's *Martyrdom of Sebastian*. In Colmar's *Madonna in the Rose Bower* in the church of St. Martin, the Virgin sits in front of a trellis rich with roses and birds, and so does Stefano de Zevio's *Madonna of the Rose Garden* in Verona. Bernardino Luini's *Madonna of the Rose Garden* in Milan's Brera, clearly shows how light poles are lashed together at right angles to form large squares over which rambles a centifolia rose. The *Madonna of the Rose Garden* sometimes called *St. Ursula's Birthday Party*, shows the Madonna and Babe seated before a low hedge entirely covered with red briar roses. Perhaps the loveliest illustration of a trellis is Vivarini's imaginative *Garden of Love* where it rises some five feet above the lovers' heads and is so thickly over-grown with flowering roses that it gives them complete seclusion.

A low trellis frequently surrounded the small herb or flower beds seen in many illustrations of fourteenth and fifteenth

This detail of the
Madonna of the Rose
Bower clearly shows
the manner in which
square trellis was tied
together and supported
a climbing centifolia
rose. Bernardino Luini,
Pinacoteca di Brera,
Milan.

A fifteenth century
Flemish illustration
shows a successful lover
about to pick a rose of a
size most gardeners would
like to achieve.

76

A Roman garden scheme included a charming suggestion for trellis-work with curves, shady roofed areas, flower-filled urns and delightful out-of-scale birds.

century gardens. Petrarch, who was an enthusiastic gardener, used a trellis to divide his garden in Parma in two, the first section devoted to vegetables and herbs, the second a pleasure garden with a flower-sprinkled lawn and fruit trees over which he grew vines, in spite of the protests of contemporary garden specialists who deplored this practice. Petrarch corresponded on garden subjects with the despot of Milan, Giovanni Visconti, who in his more peaceful moments liked to take his meals out-of-doors, shielded from the sun by a vine-covered trellis.

By the sixteenth century the trellis had crossed the Alps and became increasingly popular in Holland, France and England where the earliest-known pleasure garden, made for Henry III at Woodstock, had a walled garden interspersed with fountains and arbours entirely surrounded by a trellis over which climbers were trained.

In Holland many of the small town gardens showed walls of trellis often pierced by an archway in the centre framing a statue or a doorway. A typical seventeenth century Dutch garden would have high trellis walls with a fountain in the centre where two paths crossed and with shrubs in each of the corners. The fashion for training the branches of trees, evenly planted on either side to form a shady alley, has survived to this day, and can still be seen in some sleepy, provincial Dutch towns. A traveller in the 1930's remarked on the alleys of lime trees whose branches interlacing overhead were one of the delights of the little town of Harderwijk.

Arbours composed of trees planted closely together and

77

trained to compose a summer-house were also a favourite device and many Dutch genre pictures show the burghers sitting in such arbours, or 'herbers' as they sometimes were called. Bernard Palissy, famous potter but also a keen gardener, describes such a leafy retreat in his own garden. These arbours often had turf seats usually cushioned with camomile, pennyroyal, daisies and wild violets which remained fashionable until the end of the seventeenth century. In France the trellis was brought to a high state of sophistication and developed into designs of great complexity which made it an item of major importance in garden planning. A passage-way ceilinged with a vaulted trellis or an alley or arched trees was known by the charming name of *berceau*. These pleached alleys, also called *tonnelles*, usually composed of hornbeams or wych elm, were a great feature of Tudor gardens, one of which still exists, the so-called Queen's Bower at Hampton. Such an arbour composed of cypress trees can also still be seen in the Generalife gardens in Spain but the arbour with a trellis top designed by William Chambers for Kew has vanished. These delightful devices went out of fashion after the seventeenth century though sometimes little walks of nut-trees grown in this manner still can be found in old-fashioned gardens. Endless permutations were invented on the simple theme of the trellis including elaborate *trompe l'oeil* constructions, such as those to be seen on the side and back walls of many Parisian dwellings in which false perspective, glimpsed through arches of diminishing size, cause long vistas to appear where in reality there is nothing but a flat surface. The conceit of an *oeil de boeuf* aperture at intervals in the trellis-wall was often employed, and instead of the usual straight line the top of the trellis was sometimes finished by a series of crenellations. These variations were considered as garden ornaments in their own right and not as supports for climbers which, if permitted, were restricted to various kinds of ivy, severely pruned. Many Parisian courtyards exhibit examples of such work which was greatly admired in the late nineteenth century, and together with well-raked pebbles and small begonias planted in straight rows, composed the average French town garden until the coming of the 'modern style' in the Twenties and still can be seen in hundreds of provincial towns.

Trellis work was employed not only as walls to form small pavilions, but often composed part of the house-wall where it was not intended as a mere support for climbers, as it would be in more romantic England, but as a calculated part of the design. In this country there are few examples of the trellis used purely as an architectural construction, though an interesting exception can be seen at Warren Towers near Newmarket, but in France there are many illustrations of this device. The lovely little seventeenth century Maison de Sylvie at Chantilly, which is no more than a bungalow built in stone, has its low walls covered with a square trellis on which no plants are permitted to intrude. There were several other examples of elaborate *treillage* at Chantilly, one in the form of an obelisk, another as a *Temple d'Amour,* and some so high that they composed canyons of deep shade, miniature rustic precursors of the high-rise buildings of today. The Petit Trianon contains probably the best known example of this form of decoration and its open-air dining room, or *salon frais,* had walls of trellis work. The squared trellis is obviously more suited to the symmetry of a classic building, just as the diamond shape harmonises best with the Gothick or romantic taste, but it can also be obtained in a variety of patterns. The life of such constructions is necessarily limited. They are the first casualties of neglect and it is from drawings or prints that we know of these fragile follies rather than from existing examples.

The French love of *treillage* is noticeable in many pictures of the impressionist painters, particularly Manet and Berthe Morisot, in whose garden scenes trellis backgrounds and arches throw the shadow patterns which always have been a delight to artists—as they continue to be to all beholders. The trellis has continued to be a favourite subject in Italy where it is obviously of greater interest in a land of sunlight than in the gloomy north. But the trellis-hedge is rarely seen nowadays for though their decorative value is high their upkeep is expensive and their existence short.

Except in France, the trellis was seldom seen during the period when landscape gardening was fashionable, but it returned in force with the Victorian love of decoration and became accepted as an invaluable addition to any garden which needed shade or support for some lovely climber, a special rose, a wisteria or a laburnum. The latter once-despised tree, so much admired by the Edwardians and so scornfully derided by their children, once more has returned to favour and never looks better than when trained over a series of arches to form a corridor of glittering gold. This is done to great effect in the Scotch garden of Dundonnell where the tunnel of sweet smelling golden tassels, filled with the hum of bees, provides an unforgettable experience.

The trellis became a favoured item in Victorian times and

An ingenious arrangement of square trellis surrounds the lower part of an old tree trunk at the corner of an L-shaped garden and makes room for an extra climber in Mrs. Anthony Crossley's Chelsea garden.

Loudon considered it the most suitable boundary for town gardens. He suggested that it should form passage-walls from one small area to another, just as it had done in Renaissance days and later in seventeenth century Holland. In the serious and voluble manner which characterises the writings of this indefatigable man he explains why a trellis is both the best approach and boundary to a small garden and, with the newly acquired knowledge of the telescope's visual possibilities, points out that a climber-covered trellis confines the eye and darkens the vision, thus both framing and exposing the bril-

Another view of the garden shows the studio which Mrs. Crossley built in the far right-hand corner composed of a ready-made wooden structure cleverly camouflaged by decorative trellis-work.

liance of the garden beyond. He assures his readers that such a telescopic view is guaranteed to "produce a lively effect on the spectator."

Trellis-work was revived early in this century by Harold Ainsworth Peto, architect and garden-planner, a formalist whose work was much admired by Gertrude Jekyll. He was a follower of the Italian garden tradition and attempted to bring symmetry back to the English garden, so long dominated by the romantic and landscape schools and incorporated the trellis in many of his gardens, including his own at Iford Manor, near Bradford-on-Avon.

The trellis cannot be over-praised as an adjunct to crowded suburban life for if sound cannot be excluded at least unsightly views can be rendered invisible by its means. It also can be an excellent method of correcting unfortunate proportions, and it is sometimes effective to make the trellis opposite the house higher than the side walls to counteract the excessive length of an oblong garden. A high trellis with an arched arbour at the far end of the centre wall, its opening framed in ivy and flanked by a pair of fern-filled earthenware pots will give a satisfactory focal point. If the trellis is built a couple of feet out from the wall it will give the owner two narrow strips of ground between trellis and wall, hidden from view, in which odd pots or a compost heap can be kept.

One minute London garden surrounded by ugly houses was converted into a secret retreat by the addition of a high trellis to its brick walls, clothed by ivy until an apparently solid wall of greenery enclosed the small oasis of peace, shady it is true, but private to its owner. Interest was added by a classical statue set in a trellised arch, an old well-head and a couple of urns with plants in them placed where they would get the best light: the effect was a of *giardino segreto* rather than a mean backyard.

An ingenious use of a trellis has recently transformed a most unpromising piece of waste-land into a real bower of delight. As this measures a mere twelve by eight feet and could be reached only through the garage it appeared to have no future, since both its small size and unattractive approach prevented it from being made into a garden. But its owner decided to give it a special treatment which, if only for a brief moment, would make it an annual attraction. A deep trench was dug around it, all rubble and sour soil removed and a bed filled with a load of well-manured good earth brought up by lorry from the country. In this was planted forty carefully chosen old-fashioned roses, supported above wall level by a strong trellis. The narrow space between the beds was grassed because its green made a happy contrast against the rose stems. These roses are now over six feet high and form an impenetrable tapestry of colour so that one stands enclosed in a world of roses. For upwards of a month each summer this hidden rose-bower with its green carpet is a place of pilgrimage for friends, parties are given to see this miracle of colour and scent, and during the winter months a colour film is sometimes shown, and each rose named as its exquisite form appears on the screen.

Peto also favoured pergolas, but as late as the Thirties

Gertrude Jekyll was remarking that these never attained great popularity in England. Among charming exceptions is the Edwardian example of Polesdon-Lacey where a wooden pergola supported by right-angled pillars covered by climbing roses overshadows the stone paths which intersect square flower beds. This is in a garden on a far larger scale than most modern ones but illustrates a design which is as viable and satisfactory today as it was hundreds of years ago and is capable of being reduced in size without losing its appeal. Another singularly successful nineteenth century example was that made by Mrs. F. Eden in Venice, later in the possession of the Princess Aspasia, where a vine-covered pergola was under-planted thickly with lilies which grew happily in light shade.

If the size of the garden permits a pergola built along the length of one wall, with a slanting roof supported by pillars on one side, leading to a closed end, can form both a convenient shelter and a happy link between house and garden. If the end wall can be enriched by a hedge of clipped cypress with a Spanish tiled seat recessed in the opposite corner, with above it a peach or plum tree, and beside it a bed of ever-blooming roses edged by hostas, inter-planted with snowdrops and scyllas, then a garden of year-round interest could be maintained with the minimum of trouble.

An alternative to the continuous pergola is a succession of arches over which to grow climbing plants. For this stout poles should be connected across the path by smaller rods, or an arch-way created by semi-circular iron hoops attached to the piers. This is the best arrangement for roses which like the maximum of light and air and are less happy on a closed pergola.

The climbing Jersey Beauty with its polished foliage and red hips which follow the blooms is a good choice. Albertine is difficult to rival, and the old fashioned *Felicity et Perpetue* with its pendant clusters are particularly suitable for this position, and other reliable climbers are the species *Moyesii* or *Rubrifolia*. It is a good plan to interplant one or two clematis with these ramblers, the sky blue of the Beauty of Worcester is lovely with Albertine, Nellie Moser with its large pink petals barred with mauve or the bluish-pink of Comtesse de Bouchard are good with almost any colour except red. The purple Jack-manni which is remarkably free-flowering in late summer looks best with the creamy yellow of Alberic Barbier or the large pale yellow petals of Mermaid whose leaves with their bronze tint and thick growth are a perfect foil and support for the fragile growth of the clematis. Grape vines, such as the Royal Mus-

cadine whose well-formed leaves turn a lovely colour in autumn are a must, and *V. cordate* as well as turning a low-toned red has a delicious scent. Other sweet-smelling climbers are the common white jasmine, the Dutch honeysuckle and *Forsythia Suspensa*. Wistaria is possibly the best of all flowering climbers but slow to start and impatient gardeners will require an alternative which will grow quickly and can be discarded without too many tears when the wistaria is properly established. A good short-cut is the great orange gourd, the French *Potiron rouge* which in one season will cover the supporting poles. Other quick growing climbers are the Japanese hop, convolvulus major and the Canary creeper which will give instant bloom, but beware of the tempting nasturtiums because in city conditions they attract that most horrible of pests, the black fly. *Bignonia radicans* is a good follower-on from the white jasmine and so is the blue passion flower with its curiously exotic air.

For a medium height trellis the Laurustinus family is a safe choice particularly *Viburnum Tinus* and *Viburnum Hirtum*, the May-blooming *Viburnum Lucidum* is tender and better trained on the shelter of a wall. *Garrya elliptica* produces mid-winter tassels of bloom and *Cassinia fulvida's* tiny gold-backed leaves make splendid sprays for a winter bouquet.

The sage-like *Phlomis fruticosa*, usually grown as a bush, lends itself to wall-training, aucubas are excellent for a shady position and resist town conditions, and an ivied trellis wall with giant-leaved rhubarb (*Rheum*) at its feet composes a decorative and labour-free scheme. If it is set up in a bed two bricks high from the ground this would allow for the addition of trailing campanulas in spring and pale lobelias in summer.

The true trellis, of course, is made of wood criss-crossed and nailed together either in diamonds or squares, supported by stout, strong, vertical uprights placed from four to six feet apart. In the late nineteenth century curved iron supports became popular and, once covered, are eminently practical but do not look pleasant when denuded of foliage. The trellis also can be made of wire netting in which case evergreen coverage is essential for unadorned it is definitely an eyesore, though it has the advantage of being most unwelcome to predatory pussies' feet . . . The quick-growing Irish ivy (*Hedera Canariensis*) will soon cover such an unsightly support and a mixture of the white and yellow varieties can result in a pleasing tapestry effect. Jasmine and honeysuckle are both good cover-ups which thrive in cities, and it is worth while to add at least one plant of the vine *Vitis Coignetiae* which produce in

A German country villa in the days of the First Empire made good use of single wooden palings in its gate and built-on garden room. 'Im Hausgarten' by Erasmus von Engert, National Gallery, Berlin.

85

autumn its magnificent red and yellow leaves for the last burst of colour before the dark days of winter close in.

The supporting piers of a pergola should have a definitely architectural quality preferably composed of the same material as the house, brick or stone, but masonry can be lime-washed to any colour. If oak trunks are used their diameter should be from eight to ten inches above ground, and tarred or charred at butts one foot above-ground, but are more enduring when set on squared stones a foot out of the ground, attached by an iron dowel let into the foot of the post and the top of the stones. These piers must be connected by good beams sited to opposite pairs with a roofing of thinner rods laid at intervals along the top. Trellis can be obtained in a variety of patterns or made to order to harmonise with other garden accessories.

Beneath shady borders created by trellis or pergola hostas are the best choice. They are a large family. of Japanese origin and the lily order (once called plantain lilies or funkia), and it is their leaves rather than their flowers which are their glory. The *Hosta Sieboldi* has huge glaucous leaves, somewhat heart-shaped, which are architectural in their splendour. *Hosta grandiflora* has beautiful pale foliage, and the small species *Hosta lancifolia* with its pointed curling leaves of green-edged white is delightful as a ground cover in shady places or as an edging. An absolutely fool-proof weed-smotherer is lamium, the dead nettle. *Lamium maculatum* has green and silver leaves, the variety *aureum* is golden leaved. Both need to be pinned down to the ground and for this nothing is more effective than the use of large, strong, straight hair-pins.

Not enough use is made in England of the potentialities of ivy as a ground coverage. In France it is usual for whole beds of it to be grown beneath trees where no flowers would flourish, and its obedient habit permits it to be easily trained into circular surrounds to a bird-bath or a statue, or as a ribbon along a shady path—always with the aid of a pair of clippers and a packet of sturdy hair-pins.

There is one quite large (some thirty by seventy four feet) London garden which is an object lesson in the art of non-gardening. It is heavily over-hung by trees and for years the owner struggled with roses (mildew), with flowering shrubs (stunted), with perennials which died back and with expensive annuals which damped off. Finally he decided to let the trees win and settled for a green shade and no colour. The whole area was paved, and a pseudo-exotic background provided by the fine shapes and glossy sheen of thirty fatsia and half a dozen fatshedras in front of which are many and varied hostas, several mahonias and skimmias, and a large collection of male ferns. The walls are clothed in a number of ivies. Eight plane trees down one side cast the major shade but there are also five Irish yews whose sombre green contrasts with a couple of limes and four *Ilex marsinata*. Yet, having opted for a green shade and abandoned all hope of flowers, contrariwise the garden offers pleasant surprises in all seasons. Snowdrops come first to accent the green and white theme, then in the spring the whole area is a mist of bluebells self-sown between the stones and the, as yet invisible, hostas. Then comes crocus, scillas, primroses, daffodils and hyacinths followed by drifts of lily-of-the-valley no longer impeded by annuals. In the summer pink oxalis and blue campanulas form a carpet for the architectural forms of acanthus, jasmine and clematis enrich the ivied walls and Solomon's seal continues the green and white theme.

In a (potentially) sunny position it is sometimes pleasing to create a shady covered way made of trees only—a revival of the pleached alleys of the past. This is best carried out in hornbeams, wych-elms, beech or plane planted ten to twelve feet apart, and pollarded when eight feet from the ground, their after-growth trained to a temporary roofing frame-work of poles. The same idea can be translated into a wall-covering, or a semi-solid wall to separate one garden, or section of garden, from another. An example known to all Londoners is the precinct near St. Paul's where planes have been trained to protect the idlers within from the bustle of the traffic without. Other plants which lend themselves to such a treatment are the Japanese flowering apple, (*Pyrus Malus Floribunda*), Guelder rose, Siberian and other fruiting crabs. Although in our climate shade is less a necessity than in other sunnier countries and the possibilities of the pavilion or the *ombrello* never fully explored. More attention should be paid to this subject for all too often the only suggestion offered is a golf-umbrella in strident colours, or a giant umbrella of horrible flowered cotton. Surely some variations of the charming Japanese sunshade could be devised?

For more complete shade and shelter a summer-house is an enviable addition to any garden large enough to accommodate it. Summer-houses, so quaintly referred to in the days of Charles I as 'shadow-houses', have taken many forms but the most popular was and is, a hexagonal design with an open front, two side walls pierced by windows and three solid walls at the back. This basic shape has been varied by the whims of taste: in the seventeenth century an enchanting version was designed by Robert Smythson for a garden in Chelsea with a fantastical domed roof surmounted by twin turrets, which would still be acceptable in that picturesque quarter. Another popular type is the straight fronted loggia with triple arches, the centre an open entrance with the side pierced with apertures, a formula which has been fashionable for at least seven hundred years. A charming thirteenth-century example is in the Palazzo at Rapallo where triple pointed arches frame a breath-taking view of the Bay of Salerno—an amenity forcibly lacking from urban copies but whose measurements offer sound advice to all would-be builders. The Gothic character of the walls, which encircle two thirds of the diameter with an open entrance in the centre, are in much the same style as the garden room at Gopsall Park in Leicestershire built some five hundred years later in the far different climate and countryside of western England. This, the work of William and David Hiorne, shows a tri-partite arcade with triple shaft columns and finials in the style advocated by Batty Langley in his book *Gothic Architecture improved by Rules and Proportions in many Grand Designs* which had a great influence on both houses and gardens when it appeared in 1742. Other suggestions for similar designs were for such varied styles as Palladian, Chinese and Indian, Renaissance and Baroque. These little buildings, made to delight rather than for practical reasons, are closer to fantasy than architecture but often point to important changes of taste. The Victorians also used the triple arched front but usually preferred round, hexagonal or square shapes and liked these wooden constructions to be composed of strangely twisted knotted and gnarled tree-trunks painted dark brown with creosote to discourage insects, though the latter inevitably triumphed over human precautions. A square summer-house of considerable interest is that in which Dr. Johnson used to retreat when he was staying with the Thrales and which, made of timber with a thatched roof, has been restored and re-erected at Kenwood.

When Peto re-introduced the classical style he built in his own garden a loggia, called the Casita, with a triple arched façade supported by two pairs of thirteenth-century twin columns of pink Verona marble—these latter would be impossible to procure now-a-days but the shape and proportions of this delightful little building with its low balustrade, side walls broken by small windows with sufficient space behind for storing unsightly tools and a working table would be perfect at the end of a town garden.

Another example of wooden paling encloses a tiny garden with a shell fountain as a centre-piece, furnished with simple ironwork chairs and table for outdoor eating.

Both types of summer-houses have vanished from the contemporary scene though a few, after a long period of neglect have enjoyed a mild revival, together with other Victoriana, but the average shelter today is made of sterner stuff and simpler design.

The severe economy of line admired in the Twenties, when the Corbusier-Gropius aligned groups of architects who scorned both fantasy and bourgeois comfort, deprived the garden of any sheltering summer-house. The mechanical age had arrived in the garden, and a wooden chalet on a turn-table was devised as a shelter from wind, rain or exposure to the sun, an invention more practical than pleasing to the eye.

Most summer-houses today are composed of western red cedar and are bought ready-made but can be obtained in a number of various shapes. If one is to be built to a special design it is important that the floor, best made of bricks, stone or flint, should be on a slightly higher level than the surrounding ground, not only for good drainage but also for an improved appearance.

In the past many summer-houses were thatched but during the years between the two World Wars the ancient craft of thatching almost died out. Now it is being revived and in East Anglia thatching roofs is once more a thriving business. Despite mechanisation many farmers still like to have a thatched rick and some still show a 'dolly', a small figure in plaited straw which crowns the rick and was considered to be a protective spirit. These 'dollies' are now favourite tourist mementoes and eagerly sought after. In Norfolk many thatchers cut reeds from neighbouring swampy areas but usually straw is used and, in some places, heather. The latter makes a firm and most attractive roof to a summer-house which blends in well with the green of surrounding trees. Thatching is far more durable than usually supposed, half a century may be hoped for but a quarter confidently expected. Alas, it may be difficult in urban districts to find a practitioner of this ancient craft and the roof is usually of unromantic tiles but if these can be of oak the pleasure of their silvery sheen will soon cause their cost to be forgotten. A weather-vane on the roof makes an added attraction and an opportunity to find, or commission, an original figure. A built-in seat inside the house can have a cupboard beneath it which is useful for the storage of garden odds and ends, foam cushions, etc., but it is important to ensure that this has adequate ventilation. Sliding window-screens in the Japanese manner would be a good addition for the English climate and if the construction employs both brick and stone the contrast of texture and colour offers a pleasing variety of tones.

GREENHOUSES, GROTTOES AND FOLLIES

As in the case of all fashions, whether in dress, food or flowers, several causes appeared simultaneously to make the glasshouse a popular addition to the house and garden. The improvement in glass construction, the development of wrought-iron-work, the rise of a wealthy middle-class, the increased communications with India and the Far East which brought to England scores of tropical plants, conspired to launch the greenhouse on a rising tide of popularity in the early decades of the nineteenth century which did not recede until after the first World War. Then, with a new simplicity becoming fashionable, with servants diminishing in number and the daughters taking up careers instead of whiling away the days at home, the greenhouse declined into a grimy adjunct at the back of innumerable houses, uncared for and unheated.

Linnaeus delightfully described the greenhouse as the garden of Adonis, referring to the various seeds which were sown and carefully fostered as part of the ceremonies connected with that god's power to promote growth and fertility. The practice of forcing by heat was well understood by the Romans who used pits filled with fermenting dung covered with frames made from a form of mica—thus antedating the present day plastic sheeting by over two thousand years.

The first forcing houses in Europe were built to house the precious orange trees which became an essential item in the gardens of the great. Orangeries began to be built at the end of the sixteenth century in Holland and the fashion spread all over Europe, particularly in France where—as was to be expected —Louis XIV had the biggest. It was constructed by the great architect Mansart and was able to contain one thousand two hundred orange trees as well as many other tender shrubs. Nothing on a similar scale would be seen until Paxton built the great conservatory at Chatsworth for the Duke of Devonshire in 1840.

Many people today complain that all seasons are concertina'd together and all goods obtainable all the year round but in the nineteenth century at Welbeck Abbey the Duke of Portland's staff forced thousands of pots of strawberries a year, and in Jane Austen's *Northanger Abbey* General Tilney was disappointed when he had no more than a hundred pineapples from his hot houses in one season.

The early forcing houses were not of glass but made of wood, warmed by furnaces in winter and dismantled in summer to expose the plants to the sun, but already in the early eighteenth century glass roofs had been installed in some orangeries. Steam is known to have been used for heating by the end of the century and several other cumbersome methods of heating were in use, but the hot-water system was not known in England until the beginning of the nineteenth century, some say brought over from Holland, others that it was introduced by a French emigré. Certainly by 1823 William Atkinson of Paddington had evolved a successful system of hot-water heating.

Greenhouses featured in John Abercrombie's *Gardener's Pocket Dictionary* published as early as 1786, followed in 1807 by Tod's *Plans for Greenhouses*, but these were forerunners and the greenhouse continued to be a luxury available only to the rich amateur. Most glass was heavy and opaque and if plate glass was used, as it was by Paxton for the great conservatory at Chatsworth, then the largest glasshouse in the world,

The new fashion for glasshouses is illustrated in this humorous drawing which clearly shows the bedding-out, the wooden water butt and spade usual in the early years of the nineteenth century. 'The Gardener's Offering' by Rowlandson.

it was inordinately expensive. J. C. Loudon brought out *The Greenhouse Companion* in 1824 which encouraged this new fashion, but it was not until 1846 when, mainly owing to Loudon's persuasion, the excise duties on plate glass were repealed, that greenhouses became really popular. Loudon also induced manufacturers to cut the glass to standard sizes and this too helped to facilitate the building of conservatories which reached its apogee in the vast Crystal Palace of the Great Exhibition in 1851. Inevitably Victorian advocates of the greenhouse attributed moral values to its care and pointed out that such a pastime would prevent all members of the family from card-playing, novel reading and other vicious addictions during the long winter evenings.

Loudon who might well be described as the first exponent of suburban and town gardening—though he believed that 'modern gardening' had begun two generations before his own—published his *Suburban Gardener* in 1803. Many specialists thought, and think, that he had more knowledge than taste, but on his side he considered Paxton a vulgarian. Most of his work was with large country mansions and grounds which he built or improved to the owner's taste with apparently effortless care. He was an enthusiastic and erudite botanist in touch with the leading directors of botanical gardens all over Europe and travelled as far afield as Russia. He founded the *Gardener's Magazine* in 1822, compiled the first *Encyclopedia of Gardening*, was an indefatigable writer and lecturer on all gardening subjects. Above all he was the first specialist to relate the rapidly growing volume of scientific knowledge to the facts of everyday life, and to write well-informed articles which could be appreciated by the ordinary man.

Loudon should be remembered for many benefits, among them the view over Hyde Park from the Bayswater Road, for he persuaded the town authorities to remove the brick wall which then hid the Park from the passers-by and to replace it with iron railings. It is due to his imaginative ideas on tree-planting that many London squares and streets were beautified by planes, sycamores and almonds, and it is an interesting fact that the splendid lay-out of the Ladbroke area, possibly the best piece of nineteenth century town-planning that London can show, was carried out in the late eighteen thirties when Loudon's influence was at its height. Perhaps it is to him we owe the magnificent avenue of plane trees that line Ladbroke Grove, which the Council decided to cut down a couple of years ago but was successfully prevented by an unparalleled outburst of rage from the inhabitants, and also the large number of sycamores and almond trees in this leafy neighbourhood. Unlike his thirteenth-century predecessor Pier de'Crescenzi of Bologna, who divided gardens into only three classes, Loudon counted four; first an establishment which had a park and farm of not less than fifty acres; second, houses detached on all sides; third, pairs of houses; and fourth, those in a terrace-row. The twin houses he built for himself and his mother-in-law in 1822 in Porchester Terrace where they still stand, fall into the third category and are an outstanding example of good design. The houses had classical porticos and separate entrances on each side facing away from each other. The semi-circular glasshouse with its elegant domed roof stood in the centre of the façade fronting the road. Bayswater then was almost rural, certainly the dirt of coal-fires was comparatively rare, industry non-existent and diesel fumes still far in the future, so the cleaning of the glass would not present the same problem as it would today. Nevertheless it is interesting to note that all these early practitioners in glasshouse gardening talk much and feelingly of the amount of soot and dirt in the atmosphere and, to a generation painfully conscious of pollution, it is strange to find a relatively unmechanised period apparently as badly off as the present disenchanted day. The oily dust given off by countless sea-coal fires was a serious hazard to town gardening, and the fumes of gas-lit interiors made it impossible to keep cut flowers indoors. The cult of cut-flowers in the rooms, and the appearance of numerous florists' shops, were simultaneous with the development of electric light and the disappearance of the gas-jet and mantle in the early years of the twentieth century.

In the long back garden of his house, about one quarter of an acre which contained a large glasshouse, Loudon boasted he grew no less than two thousand species of plants, six hundred in the Alpine house alone. The determination which managed to grow and ripen peaches, melons, cucumbers and grapes for eating, gourds for decoration and flowers for pleasure in a London glasshouse puts to shame the unadventuresome modern town gardener who rarely raises above a few dozen different kinds of flowering plants. However, Loudon admitted he spent about two hundred and fifty pounds per annum on the upkeep of the garden and greenhouses, an enormous amount of money in view of its different value at that time. Many town gardeners in the past made ingenious use of those house walls which were warmed by the flues of hot-water pipes, a practice Loudon advised whenever possible.

In early Victorian life the greenhouse played a rôle somewhat similar—but with a change of sex—to that of the garage a hundred years later. A well-to-do family had its heated conservatory in which the ladies of the house occupied themselves with their stove-plants just as their male descendants later tinkered in the garage during the weekends. Both glasshouse and garage conferred a certain status and were evidence of financial security and good living.

Those Victorian citizens whose means did not permit of a greenhouse often consoled themselves with a Wardian case or a fernery: indeed Shirley Hibberd in his charming book *Rustic Adornments* asks forthrightly "who would live contentedly, or consider a sitting-room furnished, without a Ward's case?" This singularly simple contraption, to which the tea-trade in India and the rubber plantations in Malaya owe their origins, consisted of a glass case, placed over suitable soil which thus protected the plant from changes of temperature or from the

Wardian cases, originally contrived to transport cuttings, became popular adornments of those Victorian homes not large enough to contain a glasshouse.

95

fumes of sea-coal fires or the atmospheric pollution of gas. In a decorative guise of carved wood and glass it became a drawing room ornament but originally was devised as a scientific means of transporting botanical specimens. It was in Wardian cases that tea-slips from China were safely transported across the ocean to form the nucleus of the tea industry in India, and rubber plants from South America across the Atlantic to Kew, from whence they were sent to Malaya to found the great rubber plantations.

A more modest hobby than growing exotic plants was the mania for fern collecting which began in the eighteen-thirties and reached its greatest popularity twenty years later. Glass cases were built both to stand in the room or specially constructed wooden boxes were made to be placed either inside the window or on the outer sill so that the occupants of the room looked out through a screen of greenery. The effect was very similar to the double window filled with house plants long popular in Scandinavia which has become a familiar form of decoration in this country during the last couple of decades.

The import of exotic ferns became a thriving trade and fern amateurs increased in numbers, but the majority of people contented themselves with growing as many of the native ferns as they could, either in the limited space of a fern-case or more spaciously in shady corners of their back gardens. Fern collecting became part of the Victorian mania for acquiring objects—beautiful birds, curious insects or shells—and if possible encasing them in a frame or glass box. Furthermore a faint aura of virtue surrounded the fern devotees since the belief was beginning to gain ground that plants exhaled a fresh air which counteracted the foulness of town atmosphere— thus echoing some twenty centuries later Vitruvius' advice to plant green shrubs and trees in public places because both the atmosphere and the view were beneficial to the citizens.

The most regal, and therefore the most desired of the house plants was the palm, symbol of wealth and power, a cherished addition to aristocratic drawing rooms, from the Princess Mathilde's much admired salons in the rue de Berry to Hampstead drawing rooms, until it was most extreme expression, largest audience, and its final extinction, in the Palm Courts of innumerable provincial hotels. Now it has been resuscitated and is to be seen in the smartest boutiques as well as the most elegant homes.

The hardiest and longest-lived of all house-plants was the aspidistra, known as the cast-iron plant because its constitu-

Life size statues in front of ivy-clad walls stand in either corner at the end of Hardy Amies' London garden where the architectural spikes of yuccas and a host of shrubs compose a predominantly green background.

97

tion survived all hazards of atmosphere and feeding, but, although house-plants have returned to favour, the sturdy aspidistra is not yet among the chosen many.

The preference for plain rather than fancy colours, illustrated by the fern craze, was typical of the early nineteenth century when women's dress favoured light shades and the popular flowers were pale, in strong contrast to the garish colours and vivid flowers preferred in the high Victorian era.

When green plants once again returned to favour in the nineteen twenties they harmonised well with the all-white schemes of a period in which functionalism and form were the watchwords in both house and garden. The first decorative intruders permitted in the austere scheme of the Bauhaus and Le Corbusier were the climbing tendrils of *Cissus Antarctica* and *Philodendron Scandens*, the strong forms of *Ficus Elastica*, *Monstera Deliciosa* and *Fatsia Japonica*.

A great impetus was given to the use of green plants when the Festival of Britain exhibition on the South Bank in 1951 made a noticeable feature of them both in and out of doors. The conventional summer planting of red geranium, white marguerite and blue lobelia, typical of pre-war London, was noticeably absent, and in their place stood the green, gigantic shapes of Ficus and Monstera. Form had triumphed over colour.

These, and many other, plants were set in wide, shallow containers which appeared to have no drainage. This caused much interest, and finally it was revealed that instead of soil the plants were growing in a derivative of mica, a mineral known as vermiculite, already used in the trade for plant propagation but little known to the general public. Some people deplore the artificiality of this method and some plants react to it unfavourably, but on the whole it is a sensible alternative to ordinary soil for it eliminates the possibility of pest, and of the plants dying from over- or under-watering. The last twenty five years have seen a revolution in house-plants, chiefly owing to the energy and vision of one firm which has developed an immense business in what were once little-known varieties. Among the many exotic specimens which now enrich our interiors one of the most delightful is the Calamondin (*Citrus Mitis*) a miniature tree about three feet high which smells delicious and produces doll-size oranges nearly all the year round.

After a long period of neglect greenhouses are beginning to return to favour, partly because such inventions as the automatic opening and shutting of the windows and controlled spray-

A concrete mask by Henry Moore would be a good choice for a wall ornament.

98

A long grass path bordered by shrubs in a Belsize Park garden leads to an exceptionally successful exercise in perspective. Only the white-painted Gothic wooden doorway is real, all else, the marbled passage, the arch-framed statue, is the work of the owner, Mary Adshead.

In a tiny Venetian garden the essential tool shed, in reality a plain wooden construction, was transformed into an elegant pavilion by Roy Alderson's clever use of trompe l'oeil painting.

99

watering minimises the work involved—devices somewhat similar to some of those suggested by Jane Loudon in her mysterious novel *The Mummy*. This early example of science-fiction included among its novelties a steam-plough, an idea that so much intrigued J. C. Loudon that he sought the acquaintance of the author. A mutual friend obliged and Mr. Loudon was astonished to find the novelist an attractive young woman— to whom he shortly proposed. His wife may have had the imagination to anticipate science-fiction but Loudon was equally far-seeing in a practical vein. One hundred and fifty years ago he advocated a 'breathing space' of at least a quarter of a mile surrounding London, and warned the local authorities against the loss of land fertility caused by an increase of main drainage schemes. His observant eye noted a fact too often overlooked, that gardens, like palaces require a suitably attired cast, and that the lack of well-dressed persons cause a park to appear sad and empty. Descriptions of balls and routs of the last century lead one to understand only too clearly what is so often lacking in our landscape: the correctly dressed figure which adds the right note of interest.

Jane Loudon who lived on in the Porchester Street house until she died in 1858 became after her husband's death a sort of out-door Mrs. Beeton and wrote the first gardening book for ladies only, entitled *The Lady's Country Companion*, and another with the wry title of *How to Enjoy a Country Life Rationally*.

In this field she was followed by Henrietta Wilson who in 1863 produced a delightful small book about small gardens almost in the manner, though dealing with flowers instead of animals, as her near-contemporary Beatrix Potter, illustrating her simple text by pleasing and unpretentious drawings.

The present fashion for house-plants has led to a number of ingenious inventions for the propagation and the protection of the more tender. Mini-frames, light and easily assembled, measuring only a few feet in length and only half as wide can be obtained complete with a built-in watering system and thermostatic control of heating and ventilation which obviates the necessity for constant attention. It is no longer essential to use such heavy materials as brick, wood, iron or glass. Today's practical greenhouses are composed of light steel or aluminium alloys glazed with plastic sheeting which greatly reduces weight and makes them as suitable for roofs and bal-

A giant pair of clasped hands sculptured in bronze by Auguste Rodin add to the beauty of Sir Colin Anderson's Hampstead garden.

conies as for real gardens.

Recently a most ingenious construction has been put on the market which is part-greenhouse and part Wardian-case for like the latter, it is mobile. It consists of three glass sections mounted on ball-bearing castors, constructed of light metal finished a glossy white which when closed, form a transparent column five foot six inches high and a mere three foot in diameter, but when opened gives a span of eight feet. Each section is fitted with three trays which make watering and attention to the plants extremely easy. This inventive and attractive addition to the pleasure of gardening is a British invention, not at all costly and much to be recommended for either garden, balcony or roof.

An ingenious application of the Wardian theory that moist, closed conditions are required for plant life is the use of plastic bags. These now allow the amateur window-sill gardener to be reasonably sure that a cutting put into a compost-filled pot enclosed in a plastic bag, with its neck tightly tied to a supporting stick, will root successfully.

For a normal greenhouse on a small scale the Hartley model with its elliptically arched structure, stove enamelled white, with no heavy girders and transparent to ground level can also be obtained as a lean-to not more than seven feet in length. A surprising number of tender plants can be safeguarded and propagated in these modest glasshouses which would soon repay their initial cost in the extended life of existing plants and the propagation of the new, let alone in the priceless pleasure they would give their lucky owners.

Recently a great number of greenhouses which double as extra sitting space have been added to town houses, in fact the winter-garden, so long relegated to seaside hotels, has now made a come-back, smaller than its Victorian predecessor but still offering a warm, green refuge on the coldest day. An inner skin of polythene sheeting is an excellent method of inexpensive double-glazing which can make a substantial difference in temperature. A glasshouse of ten feet by seven is sufficiently large to accommodate a family of four with chairs, a small table and about three dozen plants. One of the main problems with all greenhouses is that of keeping the glass clean which is essential to the well-being of the plants, and it is well to realise and make arrangements for this to be done before optimistically embarking on the acquisition of expensive plants. The problem of shading in summer can be solved by light, easily adjusted blinds and the messy white-washing of the glass is a thing of the past.

An outdoor ornament on the same social level as the indoor aspidistra is the gnome which was to be found in suburban gardens early in this century. The gnome's prodigious success in America is due to the following story (if we can believe the BBC who retailed it in 1971). A Swiss business man returning from a hectic trip in the United States felt so deflated by the relentless rush that he endeavoured to think of something utterly useless, but peaceful, which might help to relax the inhabitants caught up in a whirlpool of unnecessary activity. He hit on the idea of GNOMES for their small backyards. He devised a gaily painted wooden figure which he named Paul, had it made in hundreds in the Black Forest, always known for its wooden toys, got in touch with garden institutes throughout the States and sold this novelty extremely well. Soon however the market reached saturation point, he had to think again, so he invented a second figure called Peter and wrote to his customers telling them that one gnome was a lonely figure, two were better. The response was excellent and in due course almost every Paul had a Peter, but then the orders fell off. Again he had to think. This time he approached a pyscho-analyst who came up with the notion that an only child needed someone smaller than itself to look down on, instead of always looking up at adults, and that a small gnome would satisfy this need. Families with only one child were approached, and once again the response was excellent—but eventually the fashion for gnomes died out, as all fashions will.

There are three postscripts to this barely credible tale—all true. The first is that of an Englishman who so detested the gnomes he saw from time to time in suburban gardens that he would go at night and remove them, leaving a note saying if the owner felt aggrieved he was willing to send monetary compensation. The second is about a contemporary artist who has become so addicted to gnomes that he collects them and hopes in due course to create a 'gnomeville' in his own garden. His task will be made easier by the third anecdote: at the recent Art Spectrum exhibition at the Alexandra Palace in 1972 a group of these repellent miniature grotesques, the work of Herman Makkink, formed an admired display. The wheel has come full circle. It remains to be seen whether the artist-collector will admit these modern newcomers among his vintage gnomes.

Garden ornaments which in the world of stone have lasting qualities equivalent to those of the aspidistra in the vegetable kingdom are those composed of Coade stone. Artificial stone had been advocated in England as long ago as 1722 when Richard Holt took out a patent for a technical discovery which, he states, was similar to the process used by the ancients, of which the secret had been lost for centuries. This remarkable material was developed by George Coade who settled in Lambeth in 1769 but died the following year, when the business continued to thrive under his wife and later his daughter, also known as Mrs. Coade. There is no doubt as to the excellent lasting qualities of Coade stone and those examples which have survived the vandalism of our 'developers' are in a far better state of repair than their real stone contemporaries. Most of the modelling of the Coade pieces, figures, groups of both human and animal figures, gods and goddesses was done by John Bacon and continued to be copied long after his death in 1799. Some of his pieces were extremely ambitious and included a river-god nine feet high and a pysche fitted up with spring-tubes for lights, as well as balustrades, rustic stones and archways. Wyatt, Robert Adam, John Nash and other discriminating architects used Coade pieces for ornaments to gateways, balustrades, archways and garden furniture. Later on fashion changed, money was scarce after the Napoleonic wars, the new cast-iron garden furniture was cheaper than Coade stone, the business declined and closed in 1830—and with it the knowledge of the secret process was lost.

The best known existing examples of this virtually indestructible material is the huge lion which now stands beside County Hall on the south side of Waterloo bridge, London but which formerly was the pride of the Lion Brewery on Victoria Embankment, near the site of the original Coade factory. Other familiar examples are the rampart figures of a lion and unicorn on either side of the carriage-way leading from Kensington High Street to Kensington Palace, and the Royal Arms on the Imperial War Museum. The figure of Nelson at Yarmouth, the great screen designed by Wyatt in St. George's Chapel and the caryatids on the porticos of St. Pancras are other examples. Coade stone urns and figures turn up from time to time in sales-rooms and anyone lucky enough to find one can be sure of having acquired an object of truly lasting value. There are

*Above left: two contrasting wooden seats:
the rustic fashion beloved of the Victorians
with monstrously curved trunks forming
the back and sides, and the sober style
favoured by Lutyens and Gertrude Jekyll
in the early years of this century.*

Facing page and above: the latter half of the nineteenth century saw an immense development in cast and wrought-iron manufacture which made possible such elaborate work as these garden seats whose backs were made in the form of ferns, flowers, or leaves. Inevitably there was a reaction against such exuberance and simple designs of plain rods and simple curves later became popular.

now many alternatives to the unlovable gnome or the familiar classical figure and sphinxes, lion's heads and Napoleonic eagles are among the available shapes. One inventive artist, Carol Taylor, trained as a furniture designer but who is now both potter and sculptor, concentrates on the theme of animals, mythical or naturalistic, and makes concrete casts sometimes painted in imaginative coloured patterns. A fantastic sphinx with curled tail and feathered wings covered with brilliant flowers can also be obtained in plain grey, and *papier mâché* ducks with naturalistic plumage or pebbles painted with surrealist fish are provided for the side of a pool.

How many of our delights are due to the spectre of boredom which has always haunted man? To combat this dire evil so overwhelmingly described by Graham Greene in his recently published autobiography, man has devised innumerable time-consuming games, but above all it is fickleness which offers an escape from tedium. Each generation discards the ideals and the outward appearances of its predecessors and, inconstancy being fairly balanced by ingenuity, manages to create new styles of costume, new shapes of houses and new ways of living.

In no department is this change of taste more apparent than in garden furniture: who of the early Twenties purists would have believed that forty years later the elaborate Victorian

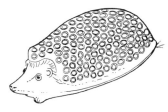

Garden ornaments (some painted) by Carol Taylor.

107

As long ago as 1754 Joshua Kirby of Ipswich conceived this unusual garden filled with geometric shapes of all kinds. Some, but not all together, would enhance a modern garden which wished to dispense with labour-creating plants.

wrought iron garden seats would be admired again? Now, after becoming highly priced items in antique shops the demand has been so insistent that several enterprising firms have begun to reproduce them in dozens. Chairs, benches and tables composed of the lovely lace-like designs of lilies of the valley, convolvulus, ferns, wheat and poppies which delighted the crinolined ladies and top-hatted gentlemen of a hundred years ago, and were anathema to the shingled flappers and Oxford-bagged youngsters of the jazz-age, are now the favourite possessions of their blue-jeaned, tail-shirted descendants.

The bouncing, mushroom-shaped iron garden chair, common in France before the First World War and recognisable in several of Vuillard's garden pictures, has yet to make its re-appearance. It has much to recommend it, its buoyancy makes it more comfortable than a solid seat and its shape sheds water as easily as the proverbial duck's back.

The revulsion from the over-ornamental Victorian furniture resulted in plain wooden benches composed of slatted seats supported by strong iron frames, sometimes with legs shaped in imitation of tree-trunks, a last remnant of the craze for rustic arches and seats beloved of the previous generation. These too, are often glimpsed in the garden pictures of Vuillard and Bonnard.

Even this slight touch of romanticism was unacceptable to the sober good taste of Edward Lutyens who designed much of the garden furniture for the houses he built. Both he and Gertrude Jekyll preferred solid benches and seats of plain wood and disapproved of even a hint of fantasy such as Chinese patterns for the slatted backs. Miss Jekyll inveighed against the fashion of painting garden furniture white and thought a white seat too glaring and obvious for a garden—one of the few ideas she propounded with which the English public has not agreed. If paint had to be used, she advised a soft shade of green but preferred plain oak which weathered to a delightful silvery sheen.

The last quarter of a century has seen a revival of good design in garden furniture and once again artists of real distinction have applied their talents to designing seats and tables for outdoor use both in wood and cast-iron. A remarkably successful experiment in the use of the latter material is a garden seat designed by Edward Bawden in which echoes of Chinese Chippendale blend well with a certain contemporary austerity. Many firms now turn out acceptable wooden furniture of simple designs but far more, alas, produce objects of horrifying vulgarity.

No one yet has revived the more ephemeral fantasies beloved of the so-called Age of Reason which included such ornaments as 'Primitive Huts, Chinese Grottoes, Triumphal Cascades, Romantic Arches, Moresque Pavilions, Turkish Mosques, and Oriental Hermitages' which are among the designs included in William Wright's *Rural Amusements* published in 1790 though some of the simpler models might well offer suggestions for a small garden. One of Wright's contemporaries also suggested obelisks of red porphyry, spheres and white stone

The garden entrance to a romantic house on Strand-on-the Green has been made even more enchanting by the addition of a pair of stone pagodas, recently discovered in a neighbouring shop by its owner, the painter Eden Box (Mrs. Marston Fleming).

bears, all objects well in the mood of the 1970's but already depicted in a drawing of Joshua Kirby's in 1754 where a veritable collection of geometrical shapes is housed in a walled garden. And what could be more austerely up-to-date than Goethe's Altar of Good Fortune, a large globe placed on a perfect cube, put up in Weimar in 1777?

There is little room in the gardens of today for the follies which amused our forbears and the word has become a term of denigration, yet if it is used in its rightful sense there is

110

every reason to rehabilitate it. Folly is derived from *feuillie*, meaning a leafy arbour or small summer-house made of branches, in fact a more up-to-date version of the medieval *herber* and was in no way connected with the foolishness now associated with it.

Among the extravagances which are within the bounds of a town garden are those *objets trouvés* which were sought for and much valued by collectors in the Twenties, a mania fostered by the surrealists, particularly André Breton. Just as primitive man countless centuries ago had attributed magic and supernatural powers to strange shapes of rocks and stones so now amateurs found beauty in these natural sculptures which brought a memory of past magic into modern life.

Curiously shaped objects of wood or stone to be found in forests or on beaches were already prized in the eighteenth century when "irregular stones, rude branches and roots of trees" figured among the suggestions for garden ornaments in *The Temple Builder* of 1720. In the Thirties there was already a swing away from the severity of the Twenties and delightful fantasies are to be found in the work of Rex Whistler and Roland Pym, both keen gardeners. Today the work of the artist Felix Kelly, though no gardener, sometimes offers suggestions in a similar vein. The desire to be diverted and surprised can never be quenched for long, each period has its own form of folly: M. Emilio Terry contemplated building a folly in the form of a snail, a fantasy never carried out, but surely its contemporary equivalent is the popular restaurant in Los Angeles built in the form of a bowler hat and called the Brown Derby?

Few people today think of including a grotto in their restricted garden space, yet here is a folk art which might well be revived to the delight of many who would like to create a more permanent record of their labours than ephemeral flowers—once described by Repton as only a "sort of episode to the general scenery".

Once the main structure—and the rougher the better—is completed, grottoes require small, relatively light materials but a vast deal of ingenuity, imagination and patience. Perhaps it is this latter ingredient which makes grotto-making at present unpopular, but with the threat of increasing leisure looming before us maybe hands which have forgotten to write, sew or knit might like something to occupy them between television programmes.

Grottoes were popular in classical times and, long before them, in the early Chinese civilisation. It is not surprising

The Gothic arbour at Pain's Hill with a pointed roof but open to the air on three sides offers a suggestion for a garden room.

112

that this latter should produce grottoes formed from oddly shaped stones grouped together to give a curious and slightly forbidding aspect, for Chinese landscape drawings often accentuate the strange and the asymmetrical, but it is unexpected to find that that Greeks, addicts of order, also built grottoes not unlike the Chinese in the fantasy of their forms. There was also something of the grotesque in the Roman versions of this garden oddity, and Pliny recounts that one, composed of pumice stone, had a large hollow tree inside it which could accommodate several people.

Grottoes continued to be a feature of European gardens but were unimportant until the sixteenth century when the Duc de Montmorency commisioned Bernard Palisay to build one in his garden at Ecouen. This was such a success that Catherine de Medici commanded another from the same talented designer which, like everything he did, was entirely original. He liked his grottoes to look like huge caves with Herms or statues supporting the entrance, and painted the interiors in vivid colours, or made them of rocks, shrubs and trees with a small stream running through their leafy shade. Many of Palisay's garden designs, which followed the French love of geometry and were laid out in straight lines, had grottoes placed at the end of each walk.

The mania for grottoes reached England somewhat later and it was generally considered that Pope's grotto, built in 1718 in his Twickenham garden, was largely responsible for launching the craze in this country. In spite of all the publicity it received the poet's grotto was rather dull and gloomy, but it gave that effect of romantic melancholy which was appreciated by his generation as an antidote to the prevailing mood of cynicism and worldliness.

The fashion for the Gothic style spread to the construction of grottoes and Batty Langley's *Temple Builder's Companion* advertised "Gothic as well as natural grottoes" as desirable additions to a gentleman's garden.

The romantic movement in Germany fostered a love of such grottoes but with usual German excess exaggerated the formula and contrived such absurdities as artificial volcanoes with light effects obtained by coloured glass and other monstrous confections which lost all sense of the mysterious.

Grottoes soon had a status rating similar to that of the greenhouse in the last century or the swimming pool in our own. Immense sums of money and years of labour were expended on their construction which sometimes necessitated

The grotto at St. Ann's Hill, Chertsey, simulates the irregularities of an underground cavern with stalactites decorated by shells.

burrowing into an existing hill or building out a projection of turf or stone. In particular shell grottoes became a symbol of taste and a luxurious amenity only enjoyed by the rich and cultivated. The most important personalities of the eighteenth century, poets and society ladies, collected shells with as much enthusiasm as did schoolboys of the pre-mechanical age. The results of energetic searches on beaches at home were enriched by the addition of magnificent shells from the Orient which were brought to Europe in increasing numbers as the trade with the Far East developed, and we hear of huge baskets entirely filled with shells being acquired by shell-grotto amateurs. The fascination of the exotic took firm hold of the eighteenth-century imagination and resulted in many delightful follies composed of shells, fossils, minerals and such decorative stones as quartz and coral all arranged in elaborate and decorative patterns. The collecting, sorting and arranging of rare shells was a pleasure and a pastime for the learned and the leisured, particularly for the ladies. Sarah, Duchess of Richmond and her daughters spent some seven years in making the exquisite shell room at Goodwood, a light and airy compartment which can hardly be called a grotto. Its near contemporary, the shell room at Mereworth is a gloomy cavern of stone, where now three sides are papered, and only the remaining fourth has a shell surround to a marble fireplace with a shell-framed mirror above it, where a few strange birds and beasts, dolphins and cranes, all worked in shells, still surprise the visitor. Such fine and elaborate work, alas, is not within the compass of the modern mind attuned to instant satisfaction, but it is an enchanting reminder of a period when days must have seemed endless and time did not have a stop.

The grotto reached the zenith of its popularity in the late eighteenth century, but it was noticeable that towards the end of the century garden ornaments, follies and grottoes were not individually designed in relation to their special surroundings but were selected from pattern books. By this time grottoes and shellwork were no longer a speciality of a private residence but had gone into public life. Finch's Grotto Gardens at Southwark and the grotto in Rosoman Street, circa 1760, were familiar London sights. The mysterious shell grotto at Margate was possibly the best known in the country and is still visited by hundreds of holiday-makers. This enchanting underground cavern fell into decay but has been restored although the lustre of the many different kinds of shells which cover the walls has been dimmed by decades of gas-lighting.

It was discovered accidentally and opened to the public in 1837, and has almost as many legends as shells attached to it, for it is thought to be of ancient origin and some people with little cause but much imagination attribute to it a past as far distant as Crete and Phoenician voyagers.

Perhaps it is too much to hope that this leisurely pastime can be revived today but less ambitious grottoes and shell-work are not impossible crafts for those who love using both their imagination and their hands. At Walhampton in Hampshire a delightful grotto has been restored recently thanks to the efforts and talents of Mary Adshead. This is a real example of folk art and was formed by a retired sailor who in memory of his life and adventures at sea composed a cavern decorated in rough mosaics and shells depicting marine life and mermaids.

An example of shell work executed within the last quarter of a century is to be seen in Grosvenor Gardens near Victoria Station. These were laid out by the French after the last war as a gesture of gratitude to the British people for their hospitality to the Free French during the years of hostility. They illustrate two typical French idioms: the shell-decorated pavilion and the *broderies* of the *Grand Siècle*, but unfortunately their restricted tonality and severe design is barely noticeable between the steady stream of scarlet buses and fast moving multi-coloured automobiles, but is well worth a close examination.

ROOFS

The habit of roof-top living is an Eastern one which until recently has not found much favour in the West. The Oriental roof is an escape from the stuffy atmosphere of the house in a tropical climate, the Western roof is the townsman's wishful escape into the fresh air of which he is deprived. Among European countries Scandinavia has shown the greatest interest in the potentialities of the roof-garden as a town amenity, and it is the avowed aim of Scandinavian architects to retrieve a large proportion of the land they build over by equipping blocks of flats with roof-gardens and balconies. So successful has this practice proved that in one town in Sweden as much as seventy per cent of its built-over surface has been returned to its citizens for open-air living.

America too is very conscious of the necessity of creating as much out-door living as possible in its crowded cities and most of their high-rise residential blocks have a number of balconies and roof gardens. The utmost ingenuity is employed to make the most of a few square yards which display an astonishing variety of design varying from abstract conceptions to reproductions in miniature of a landscape garden. Penthouses atop sky-scrapers with their own terraces, miniature Baby-lonian hanging gardens, are considered the most desirable of all residences in New York. This has not been the practice in England but with high buildings rising in every city all over the country the importance of these air-borne mini-gardens is increasing, and it is a pity that the English diffidence with regard to the climate, which rejects the pavement-cafés of continental life, produces so few opportunities for roof-gardening in its new residential units.

Neither English nor French architects give this subject much prominence, though London can claim to have one of the largest and Paris one of the most original roof-gardens in the world. Some forty years ago, a startling roof-garden was created for the Comte de Bestegui above his flat in the Champs Elysées, built by the great architect le Corbusier. Here the ground was covered with a carpet of imitation grass complete with daisies, comfortable chairs disposed around a table near a fire-place with a decorative mantel piece, over which an oval window framed a view of the city beyond. Pots with plants were arranged as they would be in a drawing room and no attempt was made to grow any real flowers. Nature was even more strictly banished than in the Roman atrium, and the effect was of a roofless room in mid-air, not an attempted garden.

A London roof-garden built at much the same time is one of the largest and most remarkable in the world. In total contrast to Corbusier's creation of a pseudo indoor apartment it attempts, and succeeds, in simulating a real country garden, or series of gardens, one hundred feet above a busy shopping street. When the store called Derry and Toms was built in Kensington High Street during the late Thirties it was decided to construct a garden over the entire area of its roof, one and three quarter acres in extent. Now, four decades later, its matured shrubs, large trees and climber-covered walls make 'the hanging gardens of Kensington' indistinguishable from any ground-level gardens—only the adjacent church spire at eye level, and the fabulous views of the city glimpsed through apertures in the high walls suggest its exceptional situation.

The weight of masonry and earth was carefully distributed over the entire area which contains several gardens enclosed within dividing walls. There is a Spanish court of fountains consisting of a long water-garden, a rustic retreat where a stream crossed by a wooden bridge meanders through a thicket and a lawn where ducks and flamingoes swim and strut as if they were in the country. A gallery of twisted columns gives

An exceptional roof-garden was created in 1936 by le Corbusier and Count Carlos de Bestegui for the latter's Paris flat. The solarium, as it was called, is carpeted with imitation grass strewn with flowers and furnished with chairs, a chest and fire-place like any ordinary room. Over the mantel shelf an oval frame presents a view of the sky and the city roof-tops.

cloistered peace to one walk, and the so-called Tudor garden with its wide archways and stone-edged brick paths offers shelter. Here vines flourish and box and ilex form a basic background for perennials and summer plants and give the town dweller excellent ideas of what will withstand best the conditions of city life.

The average depth of the soil is no more than two feet six inches above a twelve inch drainage layer of loose stones and bricks, served by six drains which converge into one main outlet. Waterproofing was achieved by a bitumastic base and so far no trouble has arisen from leakage or roof penetration.

Wind, of course, is the chief enemy and the number of small sections into which the garden has been broken up helps to ensure maximum shelter. All trees and large shrubs have to be carefully staked for several seasons until their roots have developed laterally but so successful has this been that oaks, elms, large magnolias and semi-tropical palms are all well established.

Evaporation is one of the worst problems because of the

warmth generated by the building and the shallowness of the soil, and it oftens surprises visitors to see sprays and hose still working when it is raining, but nature does not always supply sufficient moisture for the unnatural conditions of a roof-garden.

The huge Kensington example is exceptional not only for its size and variety but also because it was built as an integral part of the whole construction, with the architect making all necessary provisions for weight, drainage and water-supply.

Another roof-garden sponsored by commerce was that of Harvey's Stores in Guildford's High Street, twenty years later in date and considerably smaller than its London prototype. Here, with the exception of a few places where a structural pier permitted extra weight, the depth of soil is a mere six inches so it was not possible to plant any large species and the only trees are willows set in large tubs hidden behind screens. Unlike the Derry and Toms scheme of a series of gardens in different, but traditional styles, Harvey's roof shows a single geometrical design in which alternating circles of land and water are linked by wandering paths. The somewhat Japanese effect is increased by circular stepping stones crossing the pools in which the round leaves of water-lilies repeat the circular motif. Most of the plants are shallow-rooting aquatics, such as *Iris Sibirica* and Kaempferi, various primulas, astilbes, spiraeas, hemerocallis, hostas, trollius and ferns. The flower beds are protected from the wind by five-foot high bamboo shelters and at intervals in the surrounding wall circular platforms are constructed from which an aerial view both of the garden and the town below can be obtained.

Yet another interesting commercial garden enterprise is located on a garage roof in California surrounded by high-rise buildings whose many windows now look down on a green expanse of lawn and plants. Here a most professional approach has been adopted and the labour of maintenance reduced to a minimum. Not only is there a built-in automatic irrigation system controlled by electric clocks, but the lawn and shrub areas are separately controlled since each requires different amounts and frequency of water. The entire area is composed of solid concrete covered by a four-inch layer of light-weight rock-soil in order to ensure adequate drainage, which is then piped through all five floors of the garage direct into a storm-sewer in the basement. The weight is limited to one hundred and thirty-five pounds per square foot, the rocks and boulders are of pumice and though ordinary top-soil is used for the lawns where more depth is required, as for tree-planting, a

Indistinguishable from a real garden is this roof-top in Kensington with a shady arcade supported by twisted columns, paved walks and lawn-bordered flower beds, all high in the sky over the busy street below. Created by Messrs. Derry and Toms in the Thirties it is to be maintained by the new firm which has recently acquired the premises.

mixture of fine expanded shale, peat-moss and various fertilisers is substituted. The larger trees, strategically placed over structural piers, include olives, arbutus, cork-oak, holly, magnolias, Japanese maples, flowering crabapples and cherries, some of which have grown to the height of twenty feet. Few transitory flowers are included and more lasting colour is achieved by shrubs, while a drinking fountain gives perpetual sparkle. The plan revolves round a circular lawn with a double-oval pool and curved flower beds on either side, and the cooling tower of the ventilation plant has been cleverly incorporated into an integral part of the design, forming a pleasant background to an important clump of trees.

Few private gardens can be developed with such professional expertise, but some of the suggestions for saving labour, weight and maintenance could be usefully followed in smaller, less elaborate plans.

The use of water in all three of these commercial roof-gardens is a noticeable feature for, in spite of its disadvantage of weight, it gives back so much light and colour from the sky that it greatly enhances the colourful possibilities of an ultra-urban site. A depth of only a few inches is required to give the illusion of a lake—which brings to mind the ludicrous episode when in Ludwig of Bavaria's winter-garden on the roof of his palace a lady, disappointed in the effect of her charms on the King, threw herself into the simulated lake only to find herself standing in water up to her knees but otherwise dry and unharmed.

A London roof-garden which is not high in the sky like its Kensington cousin was recently added to the Lord Mayor's residence, which is only four stories high. The Mansion House's new garden is among one hundred open spaces cared for by the City's gardeners but it is unique in its situation. It emphasizes comfort rather than contrivance and consists of two relatively small open spaces partly divided by a large chimney stack, the smaller arranged as a sitting-out area with benches and a trellised arch and the other boasts a glass house erected, not for the propagation or storing of plants but as a sitting-room for the Lord Mayor. It is a standard cedar-wood and glass construction with three sides composed entirely of glass and the fourth set against the bricks of a chimney breast, and is furnished with glass tables and cane chairs comfortably upholstered with chintz. Central heating has been installed and also a refrigerator for drinks and their necessary ice, but no telephone so the Lord Mayor knows he can compose his speeches without interruption in this roof-top eyrie. Similar wooden and glass châlets can be obtained in various sizes and shapes and it would be possible to install one on even a tiny roof and so add an extra room where every moment of sunlight could be enjoyed. A small annexe of this type outside a kitchen back-door in which herbs could be grown and plants hospitalized would be a god-send to any enthusiastic cook-gardener. No flower beds have been attempted in the Mansion House roof-garden but roses and clematis ramble over the wooden arch, and square teak containers are gay with annuals in summer

122

 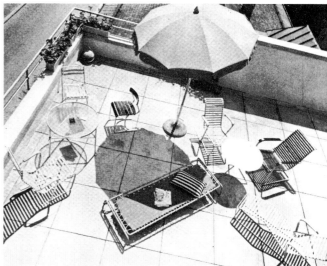

A Viennese garden laid out in the severe manner admired in the Thirties has paved and tes-sellated areas, a narrow flower bed and two large corner beds planted with shrubs. Designed by Egon Fridinges, left.

Marcel Breuer's scheme for an American apartment is in strong contrast to the fantasy of the Bestegui roof-garden. On large square paving stand comfortable but not decorative glass and metal furniture, a canvas lounging bed and sun-shade, right.

and decorative with conifers in winter.

For the amateur attempting to transform a roof into a garden the three most pressing problems are those of weight, wind and water. If the roof is not sufficiently strong to withstand a considerable amount of extra weight there can be no garden; wind offers a difficulty which must be dealt with as well as possible but can never be eliminated, only water is comparatively easy to achieve. A well-placed tap connected to the house-supply (an extra tax will be imposed) and a length of light hose is all that is needed but none the less it is a serious requirement. To carry cans of water from the house is messy, inconvenient and apt to curtail watering to an unsatisfactory minimum. Perforated rubber tubing attached to a tap can be invisible behind shrubs and will allow a small trickle of water to assure a constant watering for as long as required. Remember that evaporation will occur and that it is often necessary to water in cold and blustery weather. The idea of watering in the winter may appear ludicrous to the uninitiated but lack of it is the cause of many calamities, a week or two of fine weather, unnoticed in a cold spell, can result in total extermination of such shrubs as camellias, usually excellent and reliable town

plants, particularly if they are in pots. It is wise to tackle
the problem of the water supply before anything else is attempted and, if there is sufficient space, to build a shelter to en-
close the tap in case of frosty weather. If not to make sure
that the connections are carefully insulated.

Wind is far more difficult to deal with. It is necessary to
study the exposure of the roof and its house-wall as well as
the direction of the prevailing winds, and sometimes advisable
to build a higher wall or trellis, always provided that this does
not give undue shade to south and west exposures which are
the best for light and sunshine. Too high a wall around four
sides of an enclosure can bring with it a whirlpool of wind which
tears around causing almost as much damage as the blast
itself, and two parallel high walls can create a violent draught.
The most attractive wind-breaks are light palings, screens
of closely-bound split bamboo or compact trellis work, though
semi-opaque glass screening is attractive, far more durable
and does not require such dense coverage, and it is a good
idea to make the edge uneven, either curved or castellated
in order to break the wind and cause a less definite draught.

The difficulty with regard to weight has been greatly diminished by the new type of containers such as the Verine products
which are remarkably light and can be easily moved. Fibre
glass pots and light-weight blow-moulded polystyrene tubs can
be obtained in a wide variety of styles from imitation eighteenth century urns to conventional window-sill boxes and
contemporary abstract shapes. If the roof is a fair size and
surrounding flower borders are desired then it is necessary
to use a strong bituminous covering, though a thick plastic
sheeting, such as is used for the construction of small pools,
is a possible alternative, but unless the roof has been specially
designed as a garden and all peculiarities catered for it is better
to rely entirely on boxes, containers and tubs.

One of the great advantages of using containers rather than
building flower beds, is that each plant can be given the correct
type of soil and feeding it requires which is a considerable help
when a variety of plants are desired in a small area. Troughs
of weather-proof PVC which can be painted any colour desired,
obtainable in self-watering models both in oblongs or round
shapes, are preferable to beds in a small roof-garden—only in
a fairly spacious area should real borders be attempted and
then particular attention should be paid to adequate drainage.
If there are retaining walls around the beds it is essential to be
sure there are plenty of weep-holes in the vertical face to allow

124

water to drain away. The beds do not need to be more than two feet deep for small shrubs and plants but must have a drainage level of several inches beneath the soil.

A further alleviation of weight is the use of potting composts. Those with a high peat content such as Levington are very light but need frequent renewing and rich feeding. John Innes composts numbers two and three are very good and more permanent but considerably heavier. All the peat and loamless composts have an open texture and much soil aeration, and therefore must be carefully prepared and allowed to soak up sufficient moisture to wet them all through before planting is attempted.

In spite of the disadvantage of weight a tiny water-garden with a fountain, a dripping shell or a spouting dolphin is an addition which will give pleasure out of all proportion to the initial expense of its installation. It should be set against the wall near the house in order to facilitate the water piping and with a group of water-loving iris (*Iris laevigata*) on one side to give architectural interest by their spikes, usually about eighteen inches to two feet high. They are true aquatic plants which like their roots and the lower part of their stems in water and there are several varieties, but a deep blue is particularly appealing. Water-lilies can be counted on to amaze annually by their blooms, and will contribute an air of permanence to the ephemeral pleasure of annuals. Any water-feature such as a wall-fountain or central spray can be operated by a small electric pump circulating the same water, but this must be installed at an early stage in the proceedings in order to connect the electric lead to the pump without too much disarray. The difficulty of keeping the water clean can be overcome by the careful addition of 'Clear Water' (Algimycin GLB-X) which controls slime, algae and weed and will not harm aquatic plants or goldfish.

A miniature garden frame is a wonderful asset for a serious roof-gardener. The new type which are glazed to ground level provide maximum illumination but the wooden sided ones give more warmth. Many of the new frames made of galvanised or hot-dipped metal are exceptionally light and are equipped with easily moved windows. If a heating element is incorporated in the frame to deal both with air and soil heating the electrical consumption can be kept to the minimum by thermostatic control. With this aid tender seedlings can grow to sturdy strength before being exposed to the elements, the season of planting greatly extended and a few violet roots in a frame will

On a roof-garden in Salem, Mass., a statue emerges from a mass of shrubbery in one corner. A curbed base is planted with trailing plants and in front of it is a decorative ironwork bench.

ensure sweet-smelling flowers in mid-winter.

A lighter and more easily assembled form of plant shelter which arrives packed flat and can be put up in a few minutes looks somewhat like an oblong wigwam or small tent. It is composed of two light metal arches supported by one central and two side rods over which heavy plastic sheeting fits tightly, either fastened down the front flap with a giant zipper or partially or entirely rolled back. The makers do not include shelves but these are easily arranged inside and the whole contraption, which should be firmly attached to the roof, is about six feet high, four wide and three deep and can hold several dozen plants.

It has long been the habit of town dwellers to grow herbs in their window-boxes and one of the many advantages of a roof garden is that sufficient culinary herbs for the pot can be grown and cut when required. To be successful they should be planted in good soil loosened to at least a foot below the surface and enriched with bonemeal and rotted manure. Most herbs like full sun and good drainage, perennials should be divided or layered though some, like sage, rosemary, thyme, and tarragon can be propagated by cuttings.

An extension of the herb garden is to make the roof into a supplementary vegetable plot. Quite a small area can produce a considerable amount of salads and vegetables. The Ministry of Agriculture during the last war advised that a plot ninety by thirty feet would be sufficient for the production of all the vegetables needed by a large family, and would still leave space for bushes of soft fruit. This is far beyond the scope of any roof-gardener but even half a dozen large troughs would provide such special luxuries as the white and golden beets as well as the red, radishes both long and white and red and rosy, carrots and that useful double-purpose Swiss chard, so rarely found, whose leaves can replace spinach and whose white stalks are excellent when boiled. Kohl-rabi with its decorative leaves takes up a lot of summer space but offers a welcome change in the winter.

Of course lettuces are an obvious choice as their compact form makes them less subject to damage by wind and they are easily sheltered by light Perspex cloches. A fortnightly sowing from April onwards would save a lot of pennies. Quickly matured mustard and cress is usually a child's first foray into commerce when the green crop is cut by mother's scissors and sold to the owner of that ruined instrument for a few pence. It is best to grow cress in small square, fibre-glass containers, of much the same size as the little punnets in which it is sold in the shops, so that each crop is entirely demolished at a picking, and the pot can then be re-sown. Corn, or lamb's salad will come on after the lettuce season and continue well into the winter. Tomatoes are not to be recommended unless they can be placed in a south-facing aspect against a warm chimney-

Small statues alternate with stone flower troughs on the rim of this brick wall, recessed to admit an eating area furnished with table and comfortable chairs.

stack, otherwise their straggling appearance and unripe fruits can be a sad, and space-consuming reminder of failure. On the other hand even a small number of beans will provide from time to time a dish-full of delicious vegetables quite unlike those found in the shops. No vegetable gains more by being picked early and cooked at once than the scarlet runner which if carefully trained over a trellis is, with its red blossoms as an extra bonus, as decorative as any flowering climber. Broad beans have the advantage of being highly scented and attracting bees but the tips must be meticulously and regularly removed otherwise they quickly attract black-fly. They are rarely to be bought small enough to dispense with the tiresome chore of removing the outer covering and home-grown ones are a real luxury. Peas are more untidy and less easy but zuccinis might be attempted if the situation is sheltered. A few special kinds of potatoes could be planted such as the excellent Kipfer

East and West are dramatically confronted in this New York roof-garden where an inscrutable Oriental figure, rising from an outcrop of stones and plants, is silhouetted against a suspension bridge and the towers of some high-rise buildings.

or yellow Dutch, so valuable for salads since their flesh cuts smoothly like butter and does nor crumble and flake like the King Edwards, often the only species available. Of course the beds must be treated carefully and the crops properly rotated, with potatoes and other root vegetables followed by brassicas, peas and beans, and the soil must be top-dressed with peat, chopped straw with the addition of bone, hoof or horn meal, and must never be allowed to dry out.

Some enthusiasts go so far as to suggest bee-keeping on the roof and this is not a remote hope, more optimistic than practical for, to give but one example, a Battersea resident has for some years kept bees on his roof from which he has made honey not only for himself and his friends but of sufficient quantity and quality for it to be bought and sold by one of the most prestigious grocery firms in London. Now that town air is becoming

129

progessively purer, and birds are becoming more numerous in their escape from the insecticides and pests of the country, a rural community high in the air is a possibility for the city-dweller.

The visual appearance of the actual roof presents a challenge which is all too often ignored. The usual grey bituminous surface is extremely unattractive but provided the roof can stand the extra weight it can be hidden by superimposing thin slabs of stone paving, quarry or vinyl plastic tiles laid on a bituminous foundation. A multi-colour paving should be avoided as this will quarrel with the bricks of the surrounding walls and the colours of any flowers in the tubs, and often gives an unfortunate bathroom-like effect.

One talented roof-gardener has decorated his leads with waterproof paints in a design roughly similar to those seen on attractive Spanish rugs. This rich groundwork, on which stand camellias in pots and pansies in oblong window-boxes, adds immensely to the appearance of a small half-roof surrounded by a low trellis smothered in wistaria. A less ambitious scheme would be to paint simulated pebbles all over the plain grey surface, a feat which not all amateur artists could emulate but a plain checker board in shades of grey is comparatively easy to achieve. In some case existing roofs will have raised ribs running across them where joins in the building overlap and this necessitates the super-imposed addition of a slatted wood deck to create a firm, level and easily drained surface.

One tiny roof-haven, a mere fourteen feet by ten, with its uneven floor covered by teak duck-boarding achieves privacy by wattle hurdles covered by climbers, and stresses the division from its neighbours by an attractive statue of a seated girl at the juxtaposition of the walls. Chairs and a double-decker iron table are shaded by an iron trellis arch over which rambles a rose. Another miniscule roof-space contrived over a built-out kitchen which opens from a first floor window gives the suggestion of a room by the ingenious addition of four wooden slats placed at cornice level supported by four wooden poles, thus suggesting the enclosure of walls without their presence. Slats conceal flood-lighting which dramatises a feathery-leaved bamboo in one corner, a small shell fountain in another and a couple of chairs and a table add the possibility of a pre-dinner cocktail, or after-dinner coffee in the open. Neither of these small roof-rooms attempts any planting or demands any expensive or tiring up-keep, they are extra amenities to city living, not quasi-gardens.

A minute roof over an outbuilding made possible this tiny open-air sitting room with its creeper-clad wooden walls, slatted floor and ironwork table. The only flowers are in a few pots.

A larger London roof follows quite another pattern. Here half a dozen camellias, about twenty shrub roses, several hydrangeas, a couple of skimmias, a *Daphne odorata*, a viburnum, a ceanothus and several other shrubs form a perennial background to boxes of pansies, sweet williams, campanulas, geums, wallflowers and many annuals. Chrysanthemums and lilies appear in due season. The fragile beauty of several large fuchsias overtop a variety of geraniums and the pale bluishgrey of two eucalyptus trees contrast with the dark greens of box and ilex. This wealth of flowers and foliage is planted in large containers, single flower pots, circular wooden tubs and long window-boxes, all of which require constant weeding and

131

watering. This is no garden for an amateur roof-idler but the testing ground of an enterprising woman.

Another approximately forty-five by twenty feet belonging to a talented gardener, is approached through French windows from the living room which is on a slightly higher level so, instead of a flight of steps leading directly to the roof, the owner has built a deck platform of teak to enlarge the sitting space immediately outside the house. In the centre of this are the steps to the roof level, thus leaving on either side a space for large cupboards, equipped with pretty trellis-work doors, in which the plastic bags of compost and the many odds and ends of gardening can be stored. At one side of the steps against the next-door wall is a small lead tank covered with concrete painted stone colour in which a constant flow of water is operated by a small pump. A clever idea is the use of drain-pipes for flower pots for these take up the minimum area but give the maximum depth of soil. Climbers, such as ivy, clematis, jasmine and honeysuckle all thrive in these containers tucked into corners or placed behind shallower pots and ramble over the surrounding walls of perspex partly hidden by a diagonal trellis. On a low wall are placed shallow earthenware trays filled with rock plants and tiny succulents which do not seem to mind their rather windy position.

The average American family's response to the challenge of a roof-garden is to ignore the situation and attempt to re-create a normal garden in abnormal conditions. Trees are miraculously planted at impossible heights, stone paths lead to shrubberies, flower beds are planted with perennials and annuals, tables and chairs are available for comfortable out-door living. The small size and restricted designs of the Japanese gardens were an obvious source of inspiration for many roof-gardens and one in New York's East 52nd Street shows an excellent example of restrained rock-work, low shrubs and stone spirit house, with a great Buddha brooding over the canyon of the street below. Lawns are omitted from these conventional exercises in unconventional circumstances not because they are on roofs but because they are a luxury incompatible with the harsh American climate. Occasionally the extraordinary beauty of the situation inspires the owners to site a strange example of modern sculpture, on the edge of the abyss over which hangs the garden. The touching care which American city dwellers take of the smallest few yards of open space is symptomatic of man's longing to leave the desert he has created and return to paradise, not the one from which

132

A lesson in economy of means is illustrated in this miniscule open area, much overlooked, which relies for its effect on a wall of wooden paling and one spreading, pendulous shrub.

Pieris, yews, junipers and ivy, a tiled floor and decorative ironwork furniture compose a labour-saving background for a roof dining-room in Salem, Mass.

A small paved area contains flowers in urns, a bird-bath supported by a cherub and a thick hedge of shrubs behind which can be seen some of the surrounding skyscrapers.

his ancestors were ejected, but that which, of his own free will, he has destroyed.

To one roof-garden there are a hundred balconies though they too, are more prevalent in the southern countries than in the north. The charming habit of throwing a beautiful rug or embroidered bedspread over the balcony on feast or holy days has never reached these islands and balcony living is still in its infancy. The great blocks of flats put up in the Thirties are fortress-like in their horizontal seclusion but fortunately some of the developments of the Seventies show a different spirit and several feature a ziggurat configuration where each floor is stepped back in order to create a balcony for the flat below. The new Bloomsbury Square precinct is an example and one can only hope the new projects for the Barbican and St. Katherine's Docks will show an enlightened grasp of this amenity, so near to the hearts of many citizens of the 'great Wen' which, in spite of its habit of spreading, stubbornly attempts to retain its contact with nature. Most of these out-door city shelves are arranged not only for eating but also for that most popular pastime of the twentieth century, sun-bathing. Even town dwellers can indulge in this pursuit if they own a balcony provided it faces west or south, and measures as much as four by ten feet.

If the balcony is really tiny it is best not to clutter it with pots but to contrive flower boxes at the level of the railings. A stone coping of no more than eight inches broad will permit a built-up trough which is the best and most permanent form of balcony gardening. A Kensington example of this modest size included miniature rose bushes, fuchsias and hy-drangeas as well as many different kinds of campanulas, thrift, sweet alyssum, pinks and a host of annuals grown from seed. If wooden boxes are used be sure there is proper drainage and that drips do not fall on your neighbour below. It is wise not to attempt too much perennial planting in a limited space where everything is clearly visible at all times. Annual plant-ing, preceded by a good manuring of the soil, is best and most effective if only one type of plant is used, a mass of sweet-smelling pansy faces is far better than a few odd plants dotted in among others, or one type of hanging plant backed by one of a low-growing compact shape is effective, but the choice must depend on the colour of the house and its woodwork. Heavy evergreen climbers should not be installed on a small balcony, they will give unwanted shade in winter, no flowers in summer and hold the dust all the year round. An exotic-looking climber which is amazingly reliable in city conditions is the annual *Cobea Scandens*. Although known as a greenhouse plant it thrives out-of-doors and will cover a considerable space in one season and hold its delicate cups and saucers, mauve or pale green, well into the autumn. The Passion flower (passiflora) is less hardy but will grow well if placed against a warm wall in a sheltered position. Even one flower is worth a week's work.

Recently a great impetus to roof and balcony living has been given in Europe by developments in the South of France where the new marinas on the Mediterranean coastline are the fruit of a magnificent government scheme. The quite startling seaside towns, such as Port Grimaud, are in a man-made setting which the planners have created from a sad stretch of dull shore and made into modern resorts where waterways provide almost every house with its own mooring, and each of the flats in its large communal blocks boasts individual balconies or roof-gardens. The trend is towards a communal, out-of-doors, casual existence strikingly different to the French nineteenth-century image of dark and stuffy interiors, heavily curtained, lamp-lit and fern-adorned, so admirably and nostalgically preserved in the canvases of Bonnard and Vuillard.

There is little doubt that the roof is the garden of the future and that with the increasing loss of agricultural land for building purposes, those citizens who are amateurs of nature will be obliged to transfer their dreams and desires for rural delights from ground level to the roof. Perhaps we are about to return to the Peter Pan whimsy of tree-top living, so persistently popular in the theatre in spite of ultra-modern attractions. Are we to see the William Morris back-to-earth policy and the Rudolph Steiner method of organic healthy food developed by a new generation in the upper regions of the air? Certainly the advance in the control of the atmosphere and the consequent decline in pollution, the growing use of organic lightweight soils and the construction of synthetic light-weight containers all contribute to making roof-gardening easier. If architects and builders will give due consideration to this subject, and the public will demand and encourage the proper construction of roofs suited to the demands of a mini-agriculture, a new version of city allotments, so long an admirable part of English towns, could proliferate above ground.

ACKNOWLEDGEMENTS

p=photographer, c=copyright, o=owner
d=designer or artist.

Frontispiece: o., d. Roy Alderson, and p. 99 bottom (d); p. Bill Toomey, c. AP
Page 6: o. Staedelsches Kunstinstitut, Frankfurt-am-Main
8: Redleaf, Penshurst, c. AP
10: d. five wives of Thos. Foley 1730-50, c. Country Life
12: 57: 76 bottom: c. British Museum
13 top: Walton on Thames, 106 all, 107 top two, c. AP
13 bottom: d. Jean Canneel-Claes
19: Gamberaia, c. Mrs Marion Johnson
21: The letter, d. Tissot, o. Graves Art Gallery, Sheffield
25: d., c. Anthony Denney
26 both: 64: 65 both: p. AP
30: Al Waha, Marrakesh
31: 41: 49: 58: 89: 129: p. Molly Adams, Mendham, New Jersey
32: 69: Milles garden, Tillhör, Sweden, p. Kurt Widell (32), B. M. Bild (69)
35: 53: d., c. Kenneth Villiers
36: by permission of Kasmin Ltd
39 both: 77: from *Jardins Romains* by Pierre Grimal, p. Warcher
43: c. Fitzwilliam Museum, Cambridge
44: 80: 81: o. Mrs. Anthony Crossley, p. Bill Toomey, AP
46: 47: 48: c. Author
51 right: MARS exhibition 1938, c. AP
51 left: d. R. W. Symonds 1937
55: by courtesy of Arthur Tooth & Sons
60: o. Francis Collin, p. Bill Toomey, AP
62: Emilia's garden, c. Bibliothèque Nationale, Paris
63: Allegory of life by Giovanni Bellini, c. Uffizi, Florence
68: d. Alvar Aalto
73: d. Primrose Harley
75: c. National Gallery, Melbourne, Victoria, Australia
76 top: c. Pinacoteca di Brera, Milan
84: d. Erasmus von Engert, Nazionalgalerie, Berlin

93: a. Rowlandson, o. Henry Harris
95: from *Rustic Adornments* by Shirley Hibberd
97: o. Hardy Amies, p. Bill Toomey, AP
98: d. Henry Moore
99 top: o. Mary Adshead
101: d. Auguste Rodin, o. Sir Colin and Lady Anderson
102: d. Henry Moore, o. Sir Colin and Lady Anderson
107 lower two: d. Carol Taylor
108: J. S. Muller after Joshua Kirby reproduced from *Neo-Classicism* by Hugh Honour, Penguin Books
110: o. Mr. and Mrs. Marston Fleming, p. Bill Toomey, AP
112: Pain's Hill, Surrey, p. AP
114: St. Ann's Hill, Chertsey, Surrey, p. AP
119: d. Le Corbusier
121: c. Derry & Toms, p. Alan Richards
123 left: d. Egon Fridinger, right d. Marcel Breuer
126: 128: 131: 133 all: d., c. George Taloumis, Salem, Mass., USA